Achievement Now!

How to Assure No Child Is Left Behind

Dr. Donald J. Fielder

EYE ON EDUCATION
6 DEPOT WAY WEST, SUITE 106
LARCHMONT, NY 10538
(914) 833–0551
(914) 833–0761 fax
www.eyeoneducation.com

Library of Congress Cataloging-in-Publication Data

Fielder, Donald J., 1945-
   Achievement now! / donald J. Fielder.
      p. cm.
   Includes bibliographical references.
   ISBN 10930556-46-2
   1. Academic achievement--United States. 2. School improveent programs--United States. 3. Effective teaching--United States. I. Title.

LB1062.6 .F54 2003
371.2--dc21

                               2002029720

10 9 8 7 6 5 4 3 2

Editorial and production services provided by
Richard H. Adin Freelance Editorial Services
52 Oakwood Blvd., Poughkeepsie, NY 12603-4112
(845-471-3566)

About the Author

Dr. Donald J. Fielder has been an educator since 1968, with about 30 of those years spent in various administrative positions in Florida, Georgia, Utah, and Colorado. He has worked at the local district level, the regional level, the state level, and in the private sector. He started his career as a special education teacher and has served in a variety of administrative capacities in small, medium, and large districts and in rural, suburban and inner city systems. His public school career also involved serving for six years as superintendent of schools. Don was responsible for dramatic increases in student achievement, with students achieving at the highest levels of any district in the two states in which he served as superintendent. In addition, he was part of a team responsible for elevated student achievement in an inner city/suburban district that changed from a middle-class system to one where more than half of the students were on free or reduced-price lunch.

Dr. Fielder, who received his doctoral degree from Vanderbilt University in 1989, has authored 14 articles in national journals and publications such as *The American School Board Journal, The School Administrator, The Executive Educator,* and *Phi Delta Kappan* as well as dozens of articles and columns for the print media. He has served as a regular columnist for two newspapers where he wrote on wide-ranging educational topics. He has written a book entitled *The Leadership Teachings of Geronimo: How 19 Defeated 5000,* and he has established a consulting company that specializes in leadership training to public and private organizations of all sizes. He has presented at numerous state, national, and international conferences on a wide variety of topics. Dr. Fielder has received numerous awards including The Gravity Breaking School District Award as part of the American Association of School Administrators' study on Preparing Schools and School Systems for the Twenty-First Century.

Dedication and Acknowledgments

This is the third time I have had the opportunity to write a dedication. The first was for my doctoral dissertation, which, of course, no one but my family ever read. The second was for my first book, *The Leadership Teachings of Geronimo: How 19 defeated 5000*, which, thankfully, was more favorably received than my dissertation. *Geronimo* was a different sort of book, one meant for the mass market, and was applicable to leaders in any sort of organization. It was not restricted to one field, as is *Achievement Now!* As such, I gleaned the leadership principles I had learned during my life from many different types of sources—my family, my friends, my teachers, my mentors, and my professional colleagues—as well as from other, more learned individuals than myself who had written down their ideas regarding leadership for others to study and to expand. Of course, Geronimo was a picture-perfect example of a leader who made it easy for me to convey my thoughts to others on that elusive subject.

Achievement Now! is quite different. This is a book that combines theory and research with extensive personal experience in the field of education. As such, it is a book that could not have been written had it not been for the countless number of people in education with whom I have worked and who have influenced my thinking in the most important endeavor in which we can engage—the shaping and influencing of young minds.

My first thanks goes to a person who was then a young adolescent student named Horace who was in the very first class I ever taught—a class for the mildly mentally handicapped. Horace taught me the power that educators have as exemplars for young people and the importance of setting a good example by always following what you know is right in your heart. My second thanks goes to a host of principals that had the guts to stand up for what was best for kids and their learning—Jim Mahoney, Barbara Bailey, Theresa Buczkowski, Lew Davis, Ann Elrod,

Brian Ewert, Lynn Kintz, Kathy Malvern, Gloria Steed, Gary Strubel, Peggy Schroder and Mike Anderson. My third note of gratitude goes to a group of central administrators who had the audacity to think out of the box to find ways to benefit children—Kathie Crume, Patsy Gleason, Steve Morrison, Steve Pratt, Tracy Sutherland, Dennis Isaacson and Heidi Pace. My fourth kudos go to a small but brave group of school board members who most always knew what was best for the young minds they were charged with nourishing—Ken Balser, Susan Krebs, Javier Mazzetti, Gene Lambert, Cathy Lipsett and Floyd Northcutt. My next recognition and thanks go to a group of people who each contributed unique gifts to me—Linton Deck for mentoring me in very special ways; Roy Nichols for allowing me to spread my wings and learn about all aspects of school district operations; Mary Thurman for vesting her trust, faith, and belief in a renegade superintendent; Barbara Nicholson for convincing others that I was someone to be followed; and Kathy Singleton for being a soul mate who understands and agrees with the principles by which I live.

Next comes my shining star, my joy, my pride, the one who can always bring a tear of happiness to my eye—my son Adrian Victor Fielder and his loving, adorable, bright shining star, French wife, Cecile Bladier Fielder. Thank you Adrian for your constant belief in me, for your wonderful and continuous poetic words of support and for your constant reminders that I did it the right way by doing it my way. And thank you, Cecile for loving my son, for supporting him by living in places you would never choose to live in, and for accepting us into your life and your heart.

Finally, I can never, ever thank enough my beloved wife, lifelong partner, and best friend Dr. Dorothy Ruth Robison Fielder. There have been times when it seemed that the night would never end, and when the price for standing by my principles seemed too high to pay, but Dottie was always there providing her unqualified love and support. Our love is for eternity, and I will be forever grateful that she blessed me by wanting to become my second self.

Table of Contents

Introduction

The purpose of this book is to share methods of increasing student achievement that have been tried and found to be highly successful. There is a simple truth to these methods. They work. There are few unearthed magic bullets described in these pages that have not already been discovered and used by others. However, the blending, sequencing, and completeness of steps are unique and help lead to successful change in complicated schools and districts that in turn leads to increased student achievement. This is an important point. The sole purpose of change in schools and school districts should be to increase student achievement. Change that is not designed for this purpose is meaningless change that wastes precious time, energy, and resources.

As a practicing public school superintendent, I was vainly trying to find the answers to what could be done to increase achievement. Like my colleagues, I attended conferences and seminars, read articles and books, took college courses, and networked with some of the best minds in education. I learned many useful theories, methods, and practices—which seemed to be a piece of the puzzle—but I never encountered a complete, all-encompassing model that was proven to increase achievement. Consequently, I put together in one coherent system a series of steps that I thought would lead to that end. And it did. Dramatic increases in student achievement were the result.

Many of the elements of this system are founded in a number of theories. Others are based on educational research. Still others are based on good old-fashioned common sense. Some of these elements will work in virtually any school or district. Others are probably unique to schools or districts of common demographics. Other elements not included could no doubt improve the overall model and hence student achievement. This unified system, therefore, should be viewed as a template for others to modify for their individual circumstances. However, I am convinced that some of the elements are essential and cannot be eliminated without also eliminating any chance of increasing student achievement to any significant degree. These elements are identified within the sections dealing with those elements.

Before educators use this unified approach, they should first determine if the community in which they work truly wants to increase achievement. Although it seems to be a self-evident assumption that everyone wants to raise achievement, I have become convinced that most people who are involved in schools/ districts have other priorities that prevent a major assault on behalf of this objective. It is mainly those who are not involved in schools that have achievement as their major concern. This includes our business and government leaders and our taxpayers who do not have children in school. But as Phillip Schlechty opined in his book, *Inventing Better Schools—An Action Plan for Educational Reform*, "And if safe schools are not academically productive, then there is no reason for schools at all." Without a true commitment to increasing achievement, the methods described in this book will be to no avail.

1

Focus the Mission

The Mission Statement

Most everyone in today's world works in an organization that has an established mission. Scores of books have been written about how to properly write mission statements. Any number of professional consultants can be employed to help an organization develop or redesign a mission. Although there are a number of elements that constitute a well-written mission statement, there is one that is of absolute paramount importance. It must be limited in scope. It must clearly tell everyone including the uninformed reader what the organization is all about. It must be unambiguous in defining the central purpose of the organization. It must contain phrases or words that mean the same thing to everyone so that there is no confusion about the organization's direction.

Peters and Waterman, in their classic *In Search of Excellence*, described this mission limitation as "sticking close to the knitting." They pointed out that companies that stick close to their knitting tend to be superior performers. They elaborated that organizations that branch out somewhat but which stick close to their central skill outperform all others. To be truly effective, a mission statement must describe what an organization's central purpose is. Statements that describe only ancillary purposes merely confuse the matter.

Unfortunately, private organizations tend to be better than schools/districts when it comes to writing mission statements. If one examines the statements that the vast majority of schools/districts have, it becomes immediately clear that the statements tend to be broad in scope and too general to give the reader any real feeling for what the school wishes to accomplish. All too frequently, they have euphemistic phrases stating lofty goals that do not give direction to employees because no one can describe what you can do to achieve the goal or describe when you have actually accomplished the mission.

Consider an example. Toyota's mission is "to become the largest automobile company in the world." There is no ambiguity to that mission. Everyone knows what the company is all about and what the mission is. Even though the central mission is clear, there are many secondary sub-missions hidden within the prime mission that should be elaborated upon in a more detailed philosophy or explanation of the mission statement. For example, you must have a quality product at an affordable price with exemplary service to become the world's largest automobile company. Nonetheless, the chief mission of the company is clear.

Now consider the following examples of mission statements that I found by randomly selecting school and district Web sites:

The mission of the _____ is to develop productive citizens prepared for the changing world by providing challenging, life-long learning opportunities in a safe, healthy and positive environment.

It is the mission of the teachers, administrators, and staff of _____ to provide our students with the practical skills to succeed in our society, including the ability to use and acquire knowledge, make ethical decisions, and develop healthy self-esteem.

The mission of _____ is to meet the needs of each individual child and provide the skills needed by each student to reach his/her maximum potential.

The mission of _____ is to prepare each child entrusted to us to continue his education at other institutions of higher learning and to meet his needs in the outside world.

Although these statements sound pleasant and would be embraced by many educators, they contain goals that are ambiguous. The missions cannot be measured in any meaningful manner. The educators in these schools or districts will never know if they have produced productive citizens, if the students will later make ethical decisions, if they have met the students' needs in the outside world, or if the students reach their maximum potential. First, it is extremely difficult to even describe what these phrases mean, and it is even more difficult to measure them. Unlike the Toyota statement, which can be measured every year to determine progress toward the mission, the school/district statements cannot be measured at all. No one will ever know if they are producing what they hope to produce except by receiving anecdotal incidents/ feedback. The phrases can mean many different things to employees and, therefore, provide no direction.

Now consider this statement: "The mission of Mt. Pleasant Elementary School is to have all graduating students perform at or above grade level in the core subject areas." There is nothing ambiguous about this statement. Everyone in the school knows what his/her job is. Although a more thorough philosophy or explanation of the mission statement needs to be written to explain what the core subject areas are, or to describe how student achievement will be measured, the purpose of Mt. Pleasant is clear. The teachers know it, the students know it, and the parents know it. Indeed, anyone who reads the statement knows it.

The Values of a Limited Mission Statement

There are a number of values of a limited mission statement. First, it concentrates everyone's attention, energy and efforts on accomplishing the mission. There are no wasted efforts on other goals. There are no activities, although enjoyable and even important, that do not lead to the mission. Charles Garfield put it this way in his book, *Peak Performers:*

"Peak performers are people who are committed to a compelling vision. It is clear that they care deeply about what they do and their collective effort, energy and enthusiasm is traceable back to that particular mission." Thus, it follows that if an entire school/district is to function at a peak level, the mission must be limited so that the effort, energy, and enthusiasm of all employees are targeted and not misdirected.

When the mission is clear, it is much more likely that the mission will be accomplished. This is simply because there are no wasted efforts. Whether the objective is that of a war, or a career pathway, or a baseball team, when the mission is limited, the outcome is much more predictable. If the object of a war is to drive the enemy out of a foreign country, such as it was in Desert Storm, the ability to accomplish the mission is much greater than if the object of the war is less definable, as it was in Vietnam. If the object of a young person is to become a doctor, it is much more likely that the person will undertake the proper studies to make this happen as opposed to the person simply attending college without having a clearly defined career goal. If the mission of a baseball team is to win the World Series, it is much more likely to become a championship team as opposed to a team that wants first to make a 10 percent profit on investment per year.

The third value of a limited mission is that it focuses resources into areas where they will be the most effective. Resources are almost always limited, and they need to be carefully channeled toward the primary mission of the organization. Here is one personal example of the power that a limited mission has on controlling financial resources. In one school district where I worked, we had clearly established the mission of the district as being world-class academic excellence. When a proposal came forward from a group of active, influential, and organized parents who wanted to have funding for a boys' lacrosse team, the pressure on the district and board of education became quite intense. However, we were able to weather the storm by simply pointing to the district's mission and then demonstrating that we still had significant numbers of children who were not writing at grade level on a state-administered assessment. The position that we took was simple.

We would not expend precious dollars on boys' lacrosse as long as we had one half of our students not able to write at an appropriate level. Instead, we would use the money for increased writing instruction.

Finally, a limited mission provides a means by which everyone can measure the progress toward the mission. Everyone knows how he or she is doing. No one needs to wonder if they have accomplished the mission. In short, everyone knows the score. A friend of mine who is a professional consultant believes that this simple principle is essential for any organization to prosper. His name is Chuck Coonradt and he describes his belief in the essential nature of knowing the score in his book *The Game of Work*. He writes:

> There are three kinds of workers or players:
>
> 1. Those who know they are winning.
> 2. Those who know they are losing.
> 3. Those who don't know the score.
>
> It is a fact of life that those who keep score, whether they are winning or losing, win more over the long run. These are the people who accept personal responsibility for their own actions.

He further notes, "... measurements make work as enjoyable as play because participants have a way to win. When specific measurements are employed, it suddenly becomes possible for the employee to win."

Chuck's message seems particularly pertinent to education. As long as there is no accepted measure of the success or failure of our schools, there is no objective way to determine if we are doing our jobs properly or poorly. Without the acceptance of such measures, it is impossible to satisfy the critics of public education. Acceptance of such measures provides a way for schools/districts to win. Most importantly, acceptance of objective measurements leads to a limited mission, which leads to increased academic learning. Those of us who have worked in education know that our teachers, administrators, and staff are talented, bright and caring people. I know without a doubt that educators do not deserve the criticism that has been heaped upon them during the past 20 years. I also know without a doubt that educators can and will dramatically increase student achievement when the measurement of student performance becomes the accepted norm.

If it is true that a limited mission has these four values, then why are there so few school/district mission statements that are limited in scope? There are a number of reasons. In all organizations, and particularly in education, there are many, many worthwhile and often conflicting goals that can easily become mixed into the mission of the organization. Most educators are fully aware of, and have long complained about, the various objectives, tasks, and activities that are thrust upon education by well-meaning and well-intended people or groups that have an interest in one particular area. The schools seem to be a logical place to correct whatever problem our modern society has at the time. What better place to fix discrimination? What better place to teach that bullying is not acceptable? What better place to prevent drug abuse? What better place to teach anger management/control? What better place to teach tolerance? What better place to teach fire safety and tornado safety and hurricane safety? What better place to have children become physically fit? What better place to teach ethical values shared by most civilized people? What better place to learn to play a musical instrument or to draw or to act? What better place to learn to drive a car? What better place to teach teamwork? What better place to teach the importance of punctuality and attendance? What better place to teach civility and politeness? Most people will agree that all of these things are important. Most people will agree that the schools must be a part of helping to produce adults who possess these traits. In short, most people will agree that we must help develop the whole child.

Although this is all true, it does not follow that these are primary missions of schools. Instead, these are shared missions of our society. All of our institutions have some responsibility for these worthwhile and even critical goals. The churches, the family, the neighborhood, the military, friends, the workplace, nonprofit groups, private business, the media, and other governmental agencies all share in these common societal concerns. But, it is not the mission of schools/districts to undertake all of these societal sub-missions at the expense of the primary goal of education. No other institution in our culture is responsible for the academic development or educational achievement of our children and youth. If education fails to complete its primary mission, then that mission does not get accomplished at all. There is no protective safety net. If schools do not do their primary job, children go uneducated or undereducated.

The second reason schools/districts seldom have a limited mission is tied to the first. As just outlined, there are a host of worthwhile conflicting goals or missions that we as educators can adopt as our own. Most schools/districts choose these other missions because the educators within them are compassionate people who care deeply about others, especially children. It is common knowledge that the teaching profession pays poorly. People do not aspire to be teachers because they want to get rich and retire at forty years of age. They choose the profession because they wish to help others. It is more rewarding to teachers to console a distraught child than it is to get a fat commission. It is more rewarding for a teacher to guide a young person who has been taught hatred of racial minorities to be compassionate, understanding, and tolerant of diversity than it is for that individual to make a six-figure salary. Of course, this does not mean that those who have a sizable income are insensitive or uncaring people. It simply means that certain professions have specific innate rewards and that people naturally gravitate toward the professions that are the most reinforcing to them. It is quite natural, then, for schools/districts to adopt many of the missions that conflict with the primary mission of academic achievement.

The third reason is not as flattering to us as educators. We do not like to be measured. The teaching profession has resisted the concept of objective measurement of student achievement for decades. There are many reasons we give as to why it is impossible to measure the performance of teachers or schools or school districts. Everyone is familiar with the list: It is harder to educate children who come from impoverished homes; It is impossible to educate children whose parents do not support the schools or who do not value education; The tests are invalid and do not accurately measure students' performance; Children learn at different rates; The tests we use do not measure the many different things that are taught in the classroom; Some children do not test well; The tests we use are biased against minorities; and the list goes on. There is an element of truth in all of these statements, and there is no doubt that it is much more difficult to appropriately measure the success or failure of schools than it is to measure the success or failure of private companies or other large, complex organizations. Even in publicly owned private businesses, it is becoming increasingly difficult to measure success, which typically has been defined as the ability of the company to make money and to return a reasonable profit to its shareholders. The recent Enron debacle has shown that Wall Street can no longer rely on even the largest and most trusted accounting firms to accurately account and report on the profitability of the companies they audit. The result of Enron's subterfuge was the total collapse of the retirement accounts of thousands of Enron employees who relied on their stock options to provide a critical supplement to their Social Security. This does not even take into account the billions of dollars lost by both private and institutional investors who trusted the firm's accounting practices.

The simple and unflattering truth is that most schools/ districts do not like the idea of being accountable for the academic learning of students they are charged by society to educate. This does not mean that the teachers and staff in those schools are evil people. It merely means that they are human. Most people do not like to be accountable. It is human nature to avoid accountability. We have to be taught as children to be accountable for our own personal actions. It does not come naturally for humans to want to be accountable for their actions. Most all of us would prefer to have the traffic cop give us a warning ticket instead of a speeding ticket, even when we know we were exceeding the speed limit by twenty miles per hour.

However, when it comes to others, our resistance to accountability in education flies in the face of the accountability we insist upon in virtually every other part of our culture. We demand that the automobiles we buy run properly. We insist that the glasses we purchase correct our vision. We get upset if the house we buy has a leaky basement. The computer software we use is supposed to work every time for every customer. Airplanes are supposed to land at the correct airport every time and to land on time with great regularity. As such, the large majority of people in America believe that it is reasonable to assume that most all children can learn and that schools are responsible for a certain minimum performance. Until a school/district understands and accepts the fact that a reasonable performance can and should be expected from it, and that it can measure that performance in a reasonable manner, it will never be able to accept a primary mission that is limited to academic accomplishment. And, until a school/district accepts the primary mission of schools to be academic achievement, it will never be able to significantly increase student learning.

Develop Guiding Questions

Once a limited mission statement and a more detailed philosophy are developed, a series of what I refer to as guiding questions should be designed. These are similar to the values upon which the organization is built. Many experts advise that a set of values be enumerated in order for everyone to know how to behave when the mission or philosophy themselves do not provide adequate direction in novel situations. A set of guiding questions does the same thing. The questions have the practical advantage over a set of values in that they are listed in a more useful manner. Values that are put into the form of guiding questions enable everyone in the organization to use the questions in unique situations as well as in making day-to-day decisions.

An example of one of my former district's set of guiding questions follows:

- ♦ Is this in the best interest of students?
- ♦ Is this consistent with the mission of the district?
- ♦ Will this lead to increased student achievement?

- ◆ Is the district accountable for this activity?
- ◆ Is there input from all stakeholder groups?
- ◆ Is this activity cost effective?
- ◆ Is this the best use of district funds?

It is obvious that these are value-driven questions. They are relatively short statements that can be used for everything from budget preparation to policy development. They can guide employees in both routine and novel situations. They are clear and relatively unambiguous. They can keep a district on a course it has established.

Some examples of how the questions were actually used will help emphasize their importance. This district was making budget cuts that resulted from both a shortage of funds and the fact that a close examination of the use of funds for various programs had not been undertaken for a number of years. Every program regardless of size or political sensitivity was analyzed against these seven questions. The end result was a savings of $2 million in an $80 million annual budget. These savings were later moved into initiatives that did conform to the seven guiding questions. A specific example was the elimination of funding to a program for sixth graders that sent them for a week to a mountain retreat during the school year. The program originally had many intended purposes, but over the years it had developed primarily into a social event. Upon examining the guiding questions, it became obvious to district officials that the program was not consistent with its mission, that it did not lead to increased student achievement, that it was not the responsibility of the district, and that it was not the best use of the district's funds. Based on the answer to these questions, the program was continued, but two important changes were made. First, the costs became the total responsibility of the parents who already shared a portion of these costs. Schools already had to secure sufficient funds provided by parents, including those whose parents could not afford it, to enable every child in the school to attend the mountain retreat. Second, the program's focus was changed to be academic in nature, with the objectives being directly tied to the district's learning standards. The social portion of the week would continue, but would come at the appropriate times, such as in the evenings around a campfire. The funds that were saved were then provided to schools to lower the pupil-teacher ratio during the regular school year.

Another example from this same district will again illustrate the importance of guiding questions. The district used objective data to determine if it was overstaffed in some areas and understaffed in others. Using an annual management study conducted by all of the school districts in the nearby area, the district was able to pinpoint that, in comparison to these other districts, it was the top-ranked district in custodian-to-staff ratio, while also being ranked next to last in regular classroom pupil-teacher ratio. The district was a high-growth system, which resulted in many newer buildings but few older ones. Therefore, the elevated number of custodians was not necessitated by the age of the schools themselves. The district also researched the state and national ratios for custodians and found those numbers to be consistent with the local ratios, thus confirming the fact that the district had an overabundance of custodians. Finding no other reason why the number of custodians needed to be so high, the district used its guiding questions and determined that the excess custodians were not in the best interest of the students, were not consistent with the district's mission, did not lead to increased student achievement, were not cost effective, and were not the best use of district funds. It was then an easy decision to eliminate custodial positions through a normal attrition method and to lower the ratio to be more consistent with the local, state, and national ratios. When this was done, there was very little opposition to this reduction. These two examples clearly illustrate the power of guiding questions in making both strategic and tactical decisions.

One important thing to keep in mind when developing guiding questions is to keep the number relatively small. Normally, three or four key values is the maximum. The seven that we developed in my last school district were too many. Having more than three or four key values dilutes the importance of each value, makes it more difficult for employees to truly absorb each one, and, consequently, makes it too difficult to guide their behavior. Peters and Waterman knew this 20 years ago when they noted in *In Search of Excellence*, "… the excellent companies focus on only a few key business values, and a few objectives. The focus on a few key values lets everyone know what's important, so there is simply less need for daily instructions …" The need to keep the number of values that are in turn attached to a limited mission is important. It would behoove any organization, including any school or district, to reexamine the number of values or beliefs they list as being critical and to lower the number if the list is more than the three to four I believe is the optimum number for effectiveness.

Just as every organization will have a different mission and philosophy, every organization will have a different set of guiding questions. That is as it should be. Each organization, like each community, is different from others. The important point is that a set of such questions must be developed and routinely used.

2

Increase Academic Rigor

Increase Time on Task

Common sense tells us that the more time one spends on performing a task the better one gets. Put another way, the more you practice a skill the better you get. This simple truth is seen in virtually all areas of our lives and in virtually all activities. The more you practice shooting foul shots in basketball, the more you make. The more you drive a car, the better you get at avoiding accidents. The more you experiment with a recipe, the better tasting it becomes. The same is true for formal learning. The more you hear and practice speaking a foreign language, the better you become at understanding and communicating that language. The more you write, the better the writer you become. The more you memorize the spelling of a word, the more you will remember the correct spelling.

There is nothing magical about this simple truth. However, there are qualifiers. It is also true that if you practice an incorrect way of doing something, you will simply become better at doing it incorrectly. It is also true that in many endeavors there is a plateau that an individual reaches that cannot be raised without additional extensive work, if it can be elevated at all. Therefore, there are times when additional practice only serves to frustrate and demoralize. There are times when the individual deems unworthy the effort required to improve by a small amount. It is also true that once mastery of an activity is accomplished no further time spent on the endeavor will do any good. Mastery is mastery. Periodic refreshers may be beneficial, but continual practice will not increase performance.

Recent brain research also indicates that a break from an activity is beneficial and even necessary for maximum learning to occur. Eric Jensen, in his book *Teaching with the Brain in Mind*, notes that spaced learning, with pauses and intervals for reflection, is valuable, and that without proper quiet processing time, much learning is not transferred to our long-term memories. This is especially true for mental activity. The brain appears to need a rest time filled with diverse activities to optimize learning. This seems totally compatible with earlier research indicating that unique problem-solving ideas often originate after a period of incubation in which the brain is allowed to unconsciously mull over the problem and the accompanying facts.

Although all of these caveats appear to be accurate, it does not change the basic tenet that the more time one spends on a task the better one gets. Translated into education, the more time we spend on learning, the more we learn. It is also a basic tenet that we do not have enough time in today's educational milieu. Again, these are not new notions. One of the most definitive studies published on this critical concept is *Prisoners of Time*. Reported and published by the National Education Commission on Time and Learning, which was composed of some of the same people who wrote and published *A Nation at Risk*, this study did not receive the same national attention as the earthshaking report of 1983, but contains information that is just as important. A couple of passages from the *Prisoners of Time* illustrate the point that more time is needed in our schools. The Commission noted that, "Mastering world-class standards will require more time for almost all students." They also noted that, "Finally, we find a new fiction: it is reasonable to expect 'world-class academic performance' from our students within the time-bound system that is already failing them." The Commission came to a number of other conclusions, which are interspersed throughout this chapter.

Increase Student Engagement

Before launching into the ways that schools/districts can affectively increase students' time on task, another very important caveat needs to be made. This caution does not negate the importance of increasing time on task but it is important enough to deserve special attention. Regardless of how many methods a school or district uses to increase student time on task, unless the student is actually engaged in learning during this increased time, no increase in student achievement will occur. First, this is just common sense. An elaboration of a previous example will illustrate. Even if a couple of basketball teammates who have been doing poorly the last few games on making free throws decide to stay after practice to improve their foul shooting, unless they actually practice making foul shots, they will not improve. The mere act of staying in the gym longer does not engage the players in the practice needed to improve their shooting.

In *Schools for the 21st Century*, Dr. Phillip Schlechty, who is certainly considered by many, including myself, to be one of the leading educational reformers in America, puts it this way: "What teachers and administrators can do is ensure that the school does its business right. And what is the business of the school? To produce schoolwork that will engage the young to the point that they try it, stick with it, and succeed at it. If students do this work but test scores do not improve, dropout rates do not decrease, and vandalism rates do not diminish, it may be that students are being given the wrong work." He further elaborates, " What is needed is a results-oriented management system that focuses internal attention on producing quality schoolwork for children. If this can be accomplished, test scores, dropout rates, and so on will improve...." In other words, students need to be motivated to engage in the schoolwork because it is quality work that captivates their attention. Schlechty has also written, "Students are volunteers whether we want them to be or not. Their attendance can be commanded but their attention must be earned. Their compliance can be insisted on but their commitment is under their own control." Clearly, it would do little good if we merely increased the time a student is forced to be in school. Students must be engaged more often to increase their learning.

All of this being said, it is equally important to emphasize that getting and maintaining students' attention is insufficient, in and of itself, to dramatically increase student achievement. The time that students actually spend engaged on learning needs to be increased well beyond the time that is currently provided in most of our public schools. It would be a major mistake to concentrate on only one aspect of increasing student achievement. To dramatically increase student performance, school leaders must attack as many of the factors that affect student achievement as possible, and one of the most critical is time on task.

Of course, it is easy to write about the need to increase student engagement. It is another matter to actually be able to do it. In my opinion, this is where the skill and art of teaching, and the magic of good teachers, reign supreme. We have all seen the teacher that every student wants to have, or the classroom where all eyes and ears are locked, spellbound, onto the teacher. We all like to think that we were, or are, that kind of teacher. When quality, meaningful schoolwork meets a teacher that can inspire and motivate, learning occurs in great gulps. That magic can best be learned from those that are the magicians—not from a former long-time administrator such as myself. I can only sit back and envy the art of good teaching and applaud those that practice it every day. But, as a long-time administrator and student of research, it is possible for me to share methods that schools and districts can use to provide the increased learning opportunity time necessary for increased student achievement to occur and that is what the rest of this chapter focuses on.

Determine Minimum Time on Core Areas

One of the first steps necessary to increase time on task is to determine the minimum amount of time that students should spend on the core academic subject areas. This is particularly important because this can be done without increasing costs to the school or district. Although this sounds quite simple, the actual execution is not, because you must first determine what the core academic subjects are. As soon as this discussion begins, advocates for every subject already contained in the curriculum will come forward with reasons why their area is critical and should be considered a part of the core. Understandably, most people are very passionate about their respective subjects and will do whatever it takes to protect what they view as critically important. This is simply human nature.

However, the extent to which individuals will go to protect their turfs should not be underestimated. The subjects that people teach often constitute the essence of their being. Therefore, it is natural for people to staunchly defend the importance of their subject areas. Nonetheless, the core must be defined. In most schools/districts throughout the country, the school day, year, or career is divided up between so many elements that have been stuck into the curriculum, that it is literally impossible for a teacher or school to teach them all. This has become even more apparent as more and more states turn to a standards-based education model. Not only are too many subjects or areas contained in the required curriculum, but often, too many standards are contained within the various subjects. This exacerbates the problem, and teachers, principals, or superintendents are left scratching their heads wondering how it can all get done. In fact, it cannot all get done, and that is precisely why it is critical for a school/district to determine exactly what should constitute the core academic curriculum and the minimum amount of time students will be required to interact in these areas.

The *Prisoners of Time* study came to the same conclusion. The authors wrote, "The traditional school day, originally intended for core academic learning, must now fit in a whole set of requirements for what has been called 'the new work of the schools'—education about personal safety, consumer affairs, AIDS, conservation and energy, family life, driver's training—as well as traditional nonacademic activities, such as counseling, gym, study halls, homeroom, lunch and pep rallies. The school day, nominally six periods, is easily reduced at the secondary level to about three hours of time for core academic instruction." The Commission recommended that the academic day must be reclaimed by devoting at least five and one-half hours per day to the core academic areas. They defined the core as language arts, mathematics, science, civics, history, geography, the arts, and foreign languages.

Others differ on the specific subjects that should be a part of the core, but agree that the core must be limited. Odden, co-author of *Financing Schools for High Performance: Strategies for Improving the Use of Educational Resources*, though arguing for increased staff development, points to research that shows that enrichment classes do not affect student learning in the core academic areas. He recommends dropping at least one of the enrichment classes to save money to be used for staff development. The strength of support for these enrichment areas is reflected in a statement made by Odden that when he makes this suggestion to educators "they look at me like I'm Attila the Hun."

The Third International Mathematics and Science Study (TIMSS) conducted in 1995 also confirmed that we need to restrict the number of standards we expect students to master. TIMSS compared the achievement levels of students around the world and carefully examined the practices that were used in classrooms of the various countries. What was discovered was that students in countries that outperformed students in the United States tended to have less breadth but more depth in their curriculum. For example, instead of having a vast array of mathematics concepts crammed into a text that will be covered by year's end, some of the countries with the highest achieving students spend more time studying specific concepts in detail and do not even introduce many concepts contained in the traditional American mathematics curriculum. Indeed, TIMSS found that the mathematics curricula in the United States consistently cover far more topics than is typical in other countries. It also found that the United States mathematics and science textbooks include far more topics than was typical internationally at the fourth, eight, and twelfth grades. It concluded that the preoccupations with breadth rather than depth and with quantity instead of quality probably affect how well American students perform in relation to their counterparts in other countries.

Each community will need to determine what should constitute the core of the learning they wish for students to have. This does not imply that other subject areas are not important and should be excluded from the curriculum. It only means that the areas considered to be of vital importance to the success of a person in life are those that should be considered core essential learnings. A survey conducted by the Gallup Organization for the Mid-continent Regional Educational Laboratory (McREL) and published in an article written by Robert Marzano, John Kendall and Barbara Gaddy in *Education Week* revealed some very interesting thoughts of the United States general populace. The survey asked the public what they believed was definitely necessary, probably necessary, probably not necessary, and definitely not necessary for students to learn before graduating from high school. The basis for the responses was a composite set of standards developed from an analysis of more than 116 national standards documents in 14 content areas. Based on the public's response, such a curriculum would include all of the standards in health, technology, and work skills. It would also include 50 percent or more of the standards in mathematics, science, U.S. History, language arts, civics, behavioral studies, and thinking and reasoning. Less than 50 percent of the standards in world history, economics, geography, and physical education would be included. Finally, not one single standard would be included in the arts, foreign language, or historical understanding. Of course, a survey should not determine what should or should not be included in a curriculum. However, these are data that need to be considered when determining what should constitute the core academic areas. Although there will be slight variations of the core, it will usually be composed of at least the following: language arts, mathematics, science, and social studies. Reading, writing, and communicating comprise the language arts. The content of the social studies will vary from district to district. Some districts include foreign language as a part of the core.

One critical element that the school/district must keep in mind when determining the core is what is assessed and reported to the general public through objective measurements. Although some areas may be viewed as being important, if schools are not held publicly accountable for the performance of students in the area, it makes little sense to include them in the core. For example, although music is of value to many people, including myself, schools/districts are generally not held accountable for whether or not a student learns to read music. What they are held accountable for is whether or not students learn to read. The same sort of argument can be made for the visual or performing arts, physical education, vocational education, computer literacy skills, and many other areas currently contained in the curriculum.

It is important to iterate that because a subject or area is not contained in the core academic area does not mean that it is unimportant and should not be taught. It would be a tragedy if we did not teach music, the arts, physical education, and the other areas that make life so meaningful and enjoyable. Eliminating such subjects from the curriculum would also be a mistake because they may be linked in many cases to achievement in the core areas. For example, research from the College Entrance Examination Board found that students who take four or more years of music and arts score 34 points higher on the verbal portion of the Scholastic Assessment Test (SAT) and 18 points higher on the mathematics section than students who take these subjects less than one year.

Removing subjects such as music, art, and physical education from the core means that these areas cannot be allowed to overshadow the core areas by reducing the time determined to be needed on the core. It means that they are secondary to the primary mission of the school/district. It means that they should be there to support and enrich the core but not to supplant it. This is a bitter pill to swallow for those whose lives are tied to the noncore areas. Nonetheless, it is essential to restrict the core to improve student achievement.

Analyze the Current
Time Spent on Core

Once a school/district has determined the areas that constitute the core, a determination must be made as to what percentage of the students' time must be spent in these areas. The first step to determining this is to analyze the current amount of time spent on the core. This sounds easier than it is. Each school level is different and the method of calculation will probably need to be different for elementary, middle, and high school.

For high schools, a number of methods can be used. A straight numerical approach, where the actual number of minutes a student spends per day in various subjects is counted, is one method. This would allow a school/district to compare the number of hours per day on the core that is recommended by various groups such as the five and one-half hours recommended by the National Education Commission on Time and Learning. A major drawback to this approach is that little flexibility is provided for differences that may normally occur in course selection from semester to semester or year to year. For schools/districts that have already shifted to block scheduling, which allows for more time in each class but fewer classes per day, this method may also cause problems unless a numerical average is used.

A second method for high schools is to calculate the time students spend in the core areas as a percentage of time that students spend in school each day. This is a technique that can be used fairly successfully with other school levels as well. If this method is used, it is necessary to determine the percentage of time spent in the core that would be used as the benchmark minimum required of students. This method does provide for greater flexibility than the straight numerical technique. However, there are still some of the same problems with inflexibility posed by a straight numerical approach.

A third method is to use either the numerical or percentage approach but to base the approach on the four-year career of the high-school student. Instead of looking at a daily schedule or even a semester, one looks at the entire amount of time the student will spend in the high-school setting. This provides

greater flexibility while maintaining the integrity of establishing a minimum amount of time students are required to spend
on the core. The greatest flexibility for high school comes from
using a percentage methodology applied to the number of
Carnegie units required for graduation.

Middle schools provide other challenges to correctly identifying the actual amount of time students spend on the core.
Middle-school philosophy often drives a school/district toward establishing programs that lie outside of the academic
core. Middle level is a time for exploring various interests,
choices, and alternatives. It is a time when advisory periods,
which frequently deal with nonacademic topics, are common.
It is a time when nonacademic clubs and activities have become a part of the school day because of the difficulty students
have in participating in such activities after school because of a
lack of transportation. Because of these tendencies to pull time
away from the academic core, it is important to establish a specific number of hours or percentage of time that students must
spend on the core. In the case of middle schools, it is highly advisable to count the entire school day as the maximum amount
of time available for instruction. Otherwise, the instructional
day will become so restricted with noncore activities that insufficient time will remain for academic instruction.

Elementary schools provide an even greater challenge.
Whereas many elementary schools have specialists in a number of areas such as music, art, and physical education, many
others do not. The regular teacher often teaches one or more of
these subjects in the regular classroom. When this is the case,
and often even when it is not, an interdisciplinary approach is
used. Reading is not taught as a separate subject nor is writing
or geography or art. They are all used to teach to a unit or
theme in order for instruction to be more meaningful, realistic,
and motivational. This is very appropriate. However, when
this is the case, it is still appropriate for a teacher to block certain periods of time for specific areas of instruction, even
though an interdisciplinary approach will be used. The periods of time dedicated to core areas must then have their time
increased to accommodate for the time spent on related but
noncore activities.

A more difficult problem will probably arise for a school that does have specialists for various noncore areas. Most lay people are amazed when they discover the amount of time students spend in elementary school engaged in some activity other than core instruction. Art, music, and physical education are the more traditional ones. Technology, assemblies, non-academic field trips, library time, and recess supplement them. This does not take into consideration the time students spend out of the regular classroom for more individualized instruction in special education, Title I, and ESOL. It is very rare that students miss instruction in the noncore areas to receive this specialized small-group or one-on-one instruction. Instead, the norm is for students to receive this assistance by missing part of the instruction in the core areas being taught to the entire class by the regular classroom teacher. Therefore, it is especially critical for the school/district to establish the minimum amount of time students will be expected to receive instruction in the core even if that means the students will not receive all of the noncore instruction they currently get. An average percentage method spread out over the week is probably a good way to count the amount of time currently spent on the core and to establish the minimum expectation for the future.

What is the correct amount of time that should be spent on the core? That will depend on the areas that have been defined as the core. A critical element to remember is that a school/ district probably does not presently spend nearly enough time on the core to produce world-class results. This will obviously vary from school to school and district to district. For districts that have defined the core as language arts, mathematics, social studies, and science, one gauge that has been used successfully is that a minimum of 70 to 75 percent of the time should be spent in these areas at all grade levels. This percentage needs to be increased if additional subject areas such as the arts are added to the core. Of critical importance is the fact that for students, schools, and districts with significant underachievement, this percentage will need to be higher.

In addition to the large sweeping changes that may be required to maximize the amount of time spent on the core, there are many little things that can be done. Schools/districts can examine the length of their lunch periods to assure that sufficient time is provided to eat, rest, and relax but to also assure that time is not wasted. The same can be said for recesses for elementary children. Assemblies that take everyone out of class need to be carefully scrutinized to determine their relative value compared to the academic instruction the students are missing. Too often, an assembly is held that does not provide sufficient payoff for the time missed. The same can be said for field trips. Much too often, these trips are more of a social reward than an academic outing. Unless a trip can be tied directly to the standards and curriculum, they should not be taken. The elimination of nonacademic but supposedly related activities, particularly in middle schools, should occur. For example, I have witnessed numerous Walk and Talk, John Wayne Adventures, Basket Weaving (no kidding), and Cartoon Drawing classes that the students adore but that have no connection to the curriculum. Even an examination of the number of passing periods may prove beneficial. For example, if a homeroom period is held before students report to their first period, the school has one too many passing periods, which typically take about five minutes. To eliminate the extra passing time, simply have homeroom conducted in the first period class. By using these and similar small steps, a sizable amount of time can be added to the academic core. Finding just ten extra minutes per day in these small ways would add approximately five extra days of instruction per year. This is the approximate equivalent of 3 percent of the school year.

Realign the Purpose
of Noncore Areas

The job is not finished when the school/district has modified its day to reflect longer required time in the core academic areas. The next task is to realign the purpose of the noncore areas. This means that the noncore areas should be a support to the primary mission of the school/district. They should not be conducted in such a way that the majority of time is spent on an activity for the activity's sake but should be done so that the student can be more successful in the core areas. This can be done in many different ways and many, if not most, noncore area teachers do this already.

Quality examples abound in our schools. In a traditional shop class, the task should not be for the student to complete the building of a birdhouse. The purpose should be to teach the student the mathematics skills necessary to accurately measure the wood. The object of an activity in a construction class should not be to build and fire a missile made from coke bottles but to understand the physics and chemistry behind what makes the rocket work. The same can be said for the traditional home economics class. The objective is not to cook a good tasting meal but, for example, to understand the chemistry and physics behind why water boils at 212 degrees Fahrenheit and why cornstarch thickens a broth. The object should not be only to learn to play an instrument but the mathematics behind half notes, the history of the instrument, how it is made, the physics behind acoustical waves, and the famous musicians who have played the instrument. Physical education should not be simply a matter of exercise. It should be related to health, the physiology of the body, the biological underpinnings of respiration, and how oxygen is carried through the blood stream to the different parts of our bodies. Art should not be taught in isolation of the famous artists of history, art styles, the physics of light, and the chemistry of mixing oils. Even the most ardent supporters of their respective areas often concur that there is an extensive interrelationship between their area and the pure academic areas. For example, Elliot Eisner, the creator and writer of *The Role of Discipline-Based Art Education in America's Schools*, contends that there are four disciplines of learning in art, that is, production, criticism, history and culture, and aesthetics.

This, of course, does not mean that students should not experience the pure joy of drawing, molding clay, singing a song in three-part harmony, marching in formation while playing the flute, or playing basketball. These should be enjoyed for their own sake but only after the proper academic relationships are learned. Such interrelationships build upon and strengthen the primary mission of schools/districts. Otherwise, the noncore areas become a drain on the focus of schools.

One of the reasons why this perspective is so important is that school schedules are often built around the needs of the noncore areas as opposed to the schedule being built around the academic core and the needs of the regular classroom teacher. For example, physical education teachers may very well feel that they must see students every day for thirty minutes for them to be able to teach all of the standards in the curriculum. They may very well be right. They may not be able to do their job to the degree to which it is expected to be done unless they see the students every day. However, if providing this time to the physical education program takes away from the time that has been determined to be necessary to teach the core areas, then it must not be provided. In such a case, the physical education teacher views his role as being more important than the role of the core academic teachers. The role of physical education is to support the core, and it is not supportive if the requirements detract from the primary mission of the school/district.

This realignment of the noncore areas will be fraught with much resistance. Nonetheless, it is an essential step that must be taken if academic achievement is to be improved.

Change School Schedule to Give Priority to Core Areas

It is a fact that the noncore areas of the curriculum often dominate the decisions that affect the schedule for the entire school, including the regular classroom teacher. This is especially true for elementary schools. The norm in our public elementary schools is for all children to receive training from specialists in each of the noncore subject areas. For example, it is normal for all children in the school to be taught by the music teacher. If the size of the school permits, it is also common for schools to employ their own full-time teachers for these noncore areas. This is natural. Unfortunately, this results in the direct interruption of many of the regular classrooms at a time when they should not be interrupted. In order for an art, music, or physical education teacher to see all of the children in the day they need to see to serve all of the children in the school during the week, he/she must see children from the time school starts until it stops. The net effect is that the noncore teachers take children when it is necessary for them to do so and not when it is best for children to be out of their regular classroom. In my experience, the vast majority of elementary teachers agree that the most opportune time to teach the core academic subjects, particularly language arts and mathematics, is in the morning when the children are the freshest. That is why it is universal for the regular classroom instructor to teach these core areas in the morning. Even though this is true, the regular classroom is routinely interrupted from this prime learning time to accommodate the schedule of full-time noncore teachers.

Is there a solution to this conundrum? Is it possible to offer music, art, and physical education instruction from trained specialists without interrupting the prime teaching time of the regular classroom teacher? The answer is "yes," but the solution is rarely used. One solution is to employ two or more noncore specialists for each area to provide instruction in the afternoon nonprime teaching/learning time. Of course, there are difficulties associated with this solution. It would be more difficult to hire quality specialists who would be less than full-time employees. In some cases, there would simply be an inadequate supply of specialists to fill the need. An argument could no doubt be made that this is unfair to our fellow educators and would cause them to bear a burden the regular classroom teacher would not bear. The questions that have to be answered in this case are simple ones: what is in the best interests of the students and what will lead to greater student achievement? My answer to these questions leads me to conclude that it is more important to have instruction occur in the regular classroom in an uninterrupted manner. School/districts that are serious about improving student achievement must reach the same conclusion.

The same type of logic applies to teachers who instruct in the core areas but do so at the expense of the core area time in the regular classroom. It is common for special education, Title I, and ESOL teachers to interrupt the regular classroom instruction of their students because of their own difficult schedules. This should not happen. It does little, if any, good for students to be removed from the regular classroom to receive specialized instruction if they are missing critical instruction occurring in the regular classroom while they are gone. Such teachers must view their role as supportive to the regular classroom instruction and not the other way around. It is they who must alter their schedules to see their students during noncore academic time.

Increase Length of the Day

An obvious way to increase time on task is to increase the amount of time that students attend school each day. Many studies including the *Prisoners of Time* recommend that schools remain open longer during the day. Indeed, they note that establishing an academic day for core areas requires the lengthening of the school day, both for extracurricular activities and to provide programs for students who need extra help or time to master a topic.

Many educators would agree that lengthening the day makes sense. However, there are at least as many, if not even more, educators who will argue that the school day is long enough and that students need the downtime away from school to "just be kids." The resistance to a lengthened school day can be seen in districts that have done so through the introduction of alternative programs or school models such as the Edison Schools, Inc., which typically operates an eight-hour day for students. Although one can debate the success of such programs, they have disproved the notion that children cannot attend school for a longer period of time and be able to properly attend, participate, and learn during an entire-eight hour day.

There are, of course, many reasons why people oppose a lengthened school day that has nothing to do with what is best for children. A major tenet, which must be remembered when discussing changes in any organization including schools, is that employees will support what is in their best interests and not necessarily what is in the best interest of their clients. Schools, like all other organizations, will often do what is best for the adults in the school and not what is best for the students in the school. This is simply human nature. It does not make the people in an organization "bad" people because they first view a change in light of how it will affect them. Most experts in how to lead change concur that it is a normal part of the change process for individuals to first make certain that the change will not have a negative effect on them. Only when that fear of a personal adverse effect is eliminated can the individual move forward with supporting the change. Consequently, it is important for school and district leaders to design ways to increase the length of the school day without adversely affecting those who work in the school(s). This can easily be done, again as demonstrated by models such as those used by the Edison Schools, Inc. Regardless of the impact on employees, to do what is in the best interests of students and what leads to greater achievement, a school/district should never shy away from a lengthened school day because it is inconvenient to, or not supported by, the staff.

Another problem that immediately arises in increasing the school day is a district's master contract with its unions. It is natural for people who would be required to work extra time to want to be compensated for that time. We already ask our teachers and staffs to give too much of themselves for too little compensation. However, there are ways to increase the school day for students without increasing the instructional time for teachers. Many schools have, or are shifting to, block scheduling of one form or another to accomplish this. Indeed, one can actually increase the amount of planning time teachers receive and increase the academic core instructional time for students at the same time.

Another roadblock to an increased school day are parents themselves. Many parents want their children home with them for a part of the day. They view an extension of the school day as an intrusion on their private time with their children. This runs counter to the belief that many parents like the baby-sitting aspect of school. It is true that many other parents like the idea of an extended school day as demonstrated by the popularity of school-sponsored before- and after-school day care. Like most other major reforms, there will be those who support a lengthened day and those that oppose it.

The important point is that the stumbling blocks often put forth to block an increased student day can and should be overcome. By increasing the day by 30 minutes, a school/district can increase the school year by the equivalent of 14 days. This is an increase of approximately 8 percent in instructional time per year and cannot be ignored if increased academic achievement is the mission of the school/district.

Increase Length of the Year

The same arguments that are used to support a lengthened school day can be used for a lengthened school year. Both are significant ways to increase time on task. However, there is one major difference. It takes significant new financial resources to increase the school year across the board. Nonetheless, the advantages cannot be ignored, and there are ways of increasing the school year for select populations without requiring a dramatic increase in revenues.

Once again, the *Prisoners of Time* report recommends that at least some schools in every district remain open throughout the year. They suggest that districts follow the lead of some forerunners who have established year-round programs for students who are at greatest risk or who are the farthest behind their counterparts. This should not be viewed as a way of punishing those who have not learned what others have learned. It is merely a recognition that some students take up to three to six times longer to learn the same material. Unless we provide more time on task for these students, they will forever be viewed as underachievers. They are not underachieving. They simply need more time to learn.

What funds can be tapped to increase the school year? Resources devoted to at-risk students can be used. Some schools have increased days by using Title I funds that the school/district is eligible to receive. It is important to note that there is a major difference between an extended school year and summer school. Most students traditionally view summer school, which also has its place in increasing time on task, as a negative. They know that if they were able to keep up with all of the rest of the students that they would not be inside studying books instead of outside playing with their friends. An extended school year, on the other hand, can be set up so that the calendar is spread throughout the year with shorter but more frequent breaks. At the same time, the actual number of days that a student attends can be extended. A number of year-round single-track schools have used this model for years. Even if a school district does not receive sufficient federal funds to operate a number of schools throughout the year, it should look at starting such schools with other state or local funds. The payoff for those students involved is directly related to the extra number of days students attend.

Another way to achieve such programming on a limited basis is to examine the possibility of utilizing some of the "For Profit" companies that have an extended school year as a part of their model. Such schools typically go about 20 to 25 more days per year than a typical public school. Over the course of a 13-year student career this amounts to at least one full year of additional instruction. It only makes common sense that students who attend school one full year more than the norm will learn more.

Another way of increasing time on task is to offer before- and after-school programs directly in the schools themselves. Such programs operate in many different ways. Typically they are self-sustained through payment by parents. The most favorable way to positively affect student learning is to have the program run and operated by the school/district itself. Through this approach, the curriculum of the school can be extended, thus assuring more time on the tasks the student is learning in school at the time. A second approach is to contract with private day-care centers that operate directly in the school itself. If done carefully, this approach can successfully coordinate activities in the day care that complement and support the school's curriculum. However, this approach is more fragmented and will not lead to as much increased achievement as a program operated directly by the school/district. The third and least desirable way to operate such a program is to contract with a day-care provider that is totally independent of the school and that does not coordinate the day-care curriculum with that of the school's. Although the least desirable approach, this is still preferable to not having a child in an after-school or before-school day-care program at all.

For states that provide funding for only a half-day kindergarten, another way to increase time on task is to offer a full-day program. Once again, this is a wise use of federal dollars. Students can more than double the amount of time on meaningful learning activities when they attend a full-day kindergarten program. That is a whopping 50 percent increase. For schools/districts that do not receive adequate federal funding, an all-day kindergarten program can be provided on a self-sustaining basis through fees paid by parents. Many working parents prefer their children to be in an all-day school kindergarten program instead of being at school for a half a day and at a day-care center for the other half. Once again, the advantages are that the students can be engaged in well-structured learning activities consistent with the school's curriculum taught by a trained professional. Additional funds can be charged per pupil to provide a full-day program to children whose parents cannot afford such a luxury. Every time you can offer a program where it was not offered before, student learning will increase.

In summary, though faced with significant funding problems, schools/districts can lengthen the school year by several techniques. Even when funding is not available for all schools and all children, the year should be lengthened whenever and wherever possible.

Require Regular, Consistent, Quality Homework

One of the most significant steps that a school/district can do to increase student achievement is to provide regular, consistent quality homework to its students. Once again, the *Prisoners of Time* study supports this simple, common-sense conclusion. It reports that in many of the industrialized competitor nations in Europe one-half of all students spend two or more hours per day on homework whereas only 29 percent of American students spend that much time hitting the books at night. In most international assessments, we do not perform well when compared to these countries. It is time that we look at what our competitors are doing as well as what common sense tells us.

The fact that homework extends the amount of time that students are actively engaged in learning and, thus, increases achievement, is not a new idea. It has existed for a long time as exemplified by the fact that it was identified in the 1987 publication of *What Works—Research About Teaching and Learning* by the U.S. Department of Education (USDE) as a recommended method of increasing student accomplishments. The research identified by USDE dates all the way back to 1982. The research finding states, "Student achievement rises significantly when teachers regularly assign homework and students conscientiously do it." Even then, the amount of homework American students actually did was suspect. Teachers reported assigning about 10 hours of homework per week, but students reported that they actually spent only four to five hours per week completing homework. As many as 10 percent of the students reported that they did not have any homework assigned, or that they did not complete any homework at all.

Although this concept sounds painfully simple, the implementation of a school/district policy requiring homework is not. It will probably be met with much resistance. To be sure, many people will welcome such a policy but many others will not. I have certainly encountered such resistance in every school district in which I have worked. Why? Why do people object?

Some educators argue that homework only helps the average or above-average students because they are the students conscientious enough to complete it. *What Works* disputes this. Its findings indicate that homework helps children of all ability levels and that if low-ability students complete just one to three hours of homework *per week*, their grades are usually as high as those of students with average ability who do no homework. Likewise, if students of average ability do just three to five hours of homework *per week*, their grades are usually the same as students of high ability who do no homework.

Other homework detractors point to the recent brain research and argue that students need time to be children and that if they work hard during the day at school they need the

time to rest and relax in the evenings. I certainly concur that
rest for the brain and incubation time is needed. However, I do
not believe that this translates to a dearth of homework. Rest
and incubation occur during any period when the mind is not
actively engaged in the learning task. It rests when we go
home from work or school. It rests when we watch the evening news. It rests when we practice football or ballet. It rests
when we eat. No one has determined that the rest and incubation period for the brain equates to the time school lets out at
3:00 P.M. until it takes in again at 8:00 A.M. the next morning.
The truth of the matter is that achievement increases when
students are assigned and complete homework and if a
school/district wants to increase student achievement it must
assign homework on a regular basis.

Parents and students often argue that homework takes
away from the students' ability to participate in extracurricular or out of school activities and that these activities are just as
important as schoolwork. They point out that they cannot participate in the band, attend gymnastics practice, complete pi-
ano lessons, and do homework all in the same evening. I
would agree. It is probably not reasonable to assume that a
student, even a very bright and capable one, can complete all
of those activities and do homework also. If this is the case, a
parent and student need to make choices among the various
activities. However, the school should not make that choice
for them by eliminating or reducing homework. School is *the*
job of students. It is as much their job as regular income-pro-
ducing work is for adults. As adults, we must first attend to
our job. Only after that can we extend ourselves into other areas. We cannot demand that our job be altered to meet our
other desires. We must attend to our jobs, change jobs, or face
the consequences. Students are no different. To treat them otherwise is to prepare them incorrectly for adulthood and to
cheat them of meaningful learning opportunities.

Some people argue that homework is really nothing more
than busywork which has little value. The argument contends
that unless the work can be done in class where the teacher can
monitor the work, it degenerates into mere repetition that has
little if any value. I would certainly concur that unless the

homework that is assigned assures quality engagement of students in the learning task, homework can become drudgery with little benefit. *What Works* concurs. Its research findings concluded that quality homework relates directly to class work and extends the students' learning beyond the classroom. They also found that homework that causes a student to think is more interesting and useful to the student. The point is that homework needs to be quality homework and must be given.

Why do some teachers object to homework? I am sure that there are many different reasons but we must not forget that teachers have a vested interest in whether homework is assigned and, if so, how much is assigned. That vested interest is in the additional time it takes to properly assign homework and then to properly assess the homework and to provide appropriate feedback to the student. This is not a matter of little importance. Teachers have good reason to be concerned about doing things that require even more time than they already contribute to their jobs. They put in at least as many hours if not more to their profession than most other professionals. Nonetheless, this cannot be a sufficient reason to determine that homework should not be assigned. Because of this, a policy that is established by the school/district needs to be universal and required of all teachers and students. The amount and type need to be mutually discussed and agreed upon by the entire faculty, but a default position of no homework cannot be allowed. Otherwise, achievement will be sacrificed.

There appear to be many other reasons for assigning homework to students other than the fact that it raises achievement. A number of research studies indicate that homework improves students' ability to follow directions, improves their ability to make judgments and comparisons, raises additional questions for study, and develops responsibility and self-discipline. Regardless of other benefits that homework may bestow on students, the prime factor is that homework increases the achievement of students.

How much homework is enough? One hour? Two hours? Three hours? The answer to this question is probably different for each student. Some students do work faster than others and what may be a one-hour assignment for one student is a three-hour assignment for another. Therefore, homework needs to be differentiated for students just as class work needs to be differentiated. A student who takes longer and who is extremely conscientious may need to have a homework assignment reduced whereas another student may need to have an additional assignment or an assignment that requires more in-depth work or research. The professional judgment of the teacher, tempered with parental and student feedback, must be the determining factor in the amount of the assignments. This still begs the question of how much homework is appropriate? A general rule of thumb is 10 to 15 minutes per grade level for the elementary grades. This rule changes however when a youngster moves to secondary school. At these grade levels, students are more independent thinkers and better equipped to handle a larger volume of homework. My rule of thumb for middle grades is 1.5 to 2 hours per night. For high school, the minimum should be 2 hours per night.

One other important factor regarding homework needs to be mentioned. As the name implies, homework is work that should be done at home and not at school. The common practice in the United States is for homework to be assigned and then time allowed for students to begin completing the work in class. This point was underscored by the Mathematics Benchmarking Report for the 1999 TIMSS Eight Grade study. The report indicates that "74 percent of the U. S. students reported that they began their mathematics homework during class almost always or pretty often, well above the international average of 42 percent." Although the practice of assigning work to do while the teacher can monitor the work being completed to determine if the student(s) understand the work is a sound pedagogical practice and should be encouraged, the homework assigned to the students should not be the fodder for that practice. Homework is work that should be required to be done out of class, with class time spent on direct instruction.

Schools and districts can and should engage in vigorous discussions regarding the specifics of homework. How much should be assigned? How should it be graded? What should it look like? Should it be given on weekends or vacation breaks? The important thing is that regular, consistent, quality homework needs to be expected of every teacher and every student if the school/district wants to increase achievement.

Establish Nonschool Tutorial Programs

Another area where many of our foreign competitors lead the United States in increasing time on task for students is in the amount of time students spend in tutorial type programs that are outside of the normal school day or week. Japan probably is best known for such programs. The majority of Japanese students spend additional time in such private lessons or schools, called *jukus*, thereby supplementing the direct instruction they receive from the public school. This additional tutorial assistance is so important to the Japanese that a family spends an average of $2,500 per year, per child on this supplement.

The *Prisoners of Time* study also noted the use of private tutorial programs by other countries. The report cited the fact that approximately 67 percent of the students living in Tokyo, 15 percent of all Japanese fourth graders and 50 percent of all ninth graders attend *jukus* for added instruction, remedial assistance, or preparation for university entrance examinations. These are very impressive figures.

Certainly, parents should be encouraged to use private tutors to either help their children keep up with the expectations of the school or to bolster and expand what their children are learning in school. Typically such encouragement is not given to parents unless their children fall behind in school and need special one-on-one help. Schools/districts who want to raise achievement can certainly encourage such tutoring even when the student is not in apparent need.

As we know, many parents cannot afford to pay for the help of a tutor. If the student is unable to learn the concepts with the rest of the class, or if the student needs some additional practice time with a trained guide, the student simply does not get the assistance unless it is supplied or offered by the school/district. Such assistance can make an enormous difference for students. It can provide the extra boost that a student needs to academically achieve at the levels that we should expect of virtually all students. It has the added advantage of personalizing education for the child and of providing the success necessary for the student to perceive themselves as competent, and capable academically. Although many people think that tutorial programs belong only in schools serving low-income children, such programs should be the norm in any school that has as its primary mission the increasing of student achievement. Even schools serving the most economically advantaged have children who need such assistance.

There is a plethora of ways of providing and funding special tutorial programs. The most recent comes via the federal government's Leave No Child Behind Act that requires schools/districts to provide the cost of tutoring to the parents of students who attend a school that is determined to be failing according to the federal criteria and that has been unable to improve to an acceptable level. The federal government needs to be congratulated for the tutoring provisions of this law. It can do nothing but help children who are trapped in a failed school.

There are other ways that schools can help provide tutoring services. Many schools/districts have started providing tutorial assistance via technology. This may well be the most efficient way of helping large numbers of students with the limited budgets available to schools/districts. A growing number of software programs are already available. The programs to which I refer are not the extraordinarily expensive computer-assisted integrated instruction learning systems (ILS) models that have been on the market for quite some time. The ILS models are quite good and can certainly provide a meaningful way of delivering individual tutorial assistance in a well designed structured manner. Given sufficient time interacting with ILS programs, students should significantly increase their achievement. The problem with the current programs is their expense. They are simply cost-prohibitive for most school districts. However, these are not the software programs that can have the most dramatic impact on student achievement. Because of their much lower price, software programs that are not nearly as extensive but still effective are the tutorial programs that will have the greatest impact on achievement throughout the country. Schools/districts need to do their own research at the time they are considering adding such programs to determine those they believe will best support the specific areas needing improvement for their individual school/district.

Tutorial programs provided at times other than during the school day can be provided in a variety of ways. After-school or before-school programs can be offered. Evening programs can be provided. Weekend programs can be scheduled. Programs offered in the school or in other locations in the community can be provided. Tutorial programs offered in the community churches or the boys club or the YMCA/YWCA can be developed. Special summer tutorial camps located on, or away from, the school campus can be developed. The only limit to how, when, and where such programs can be offered is the imagination.

One of the most important cost and quality factors of tutorial programs to be considered is the personnel factor. Who is going to provide the tutoring? As educators, we usually prefer to have our own trained teachers providing the tutorial assistance. However, this is usually the most expensive delivery. Quality tutorial programs can be successfully developed and operated, even though trained teachers are not the tutors. If a quality training program exists or can be developed, all sorts of people can do the actual tutoring. Retirees, high school students, military personnel, private industry employees, church groups, or parents via the PTO or other formal organization are all examples of people who may be available to tutor. In one school district in which I served as superintendent, we started a program whereby all central-office personnel were given one hour off from work time per week to tutor in the schools. This was done to provide an exemplar to others in the community and to emphasize the importance the district gave to student achievement. Nonetheless, it also provided quality tutors for real, live students. In addition, high-school service clubs are often looking for service projects they can undertake. Tutoring in a nearby elementary school, after their school day is finished but before the elementary school dismisses, is possible for high-school students in many locations.

Special tutoring programs that are operated during the actual school day are another option. However, in order for this to have the net effect of increasing the students' time on task, such tutoring must be done during the students' noncore academic time. The advantage to these programs over the nonschool tutorial programs is that they get the one-on-one help to students who cannot, or will not, come to school other than during the normal school hours.

A number of already developed tutorial programs that provide a structured sequenced way of helping students are available on the market today. Some of these are run by nonprofit organizations. A prime example of this is the Help One Student To Succeed (HOSTS) program. This program was developed in California and has been in existence for over 20 years. It was created at a time when it was recognized that many students need special mentors who can help them in a number of ways, including direct academic instruction. The success rate for HOSTS is quite high and is highly regarded by those who have worked with the program. One of the strengths of HOSTS is that a trained educator assesses the needs of the child and then gives the untrained tutor specific instructional materials to use with the student. In addition, the tutor is given some initial training as well as specific day-to-day instructions on how to use the materials given to them. In other words, they are given a brief daily lesson plan to use with their particular child.

Many locally organized and operated nonprofit programs have been developed throughout the United States. An example is The Children's Literacy Program in Colorado Springs, Colorado. This program provides one-on-one tutoring for children who are repeating first grade or for children who are in the second or third grades whose reading skills are no more than six months below grade level. The tutoring is provided by volunteers sixteen years of age or older for two hours a week for twelve weeks. The Children's Literacy Center is a success story, with 90 percent of the participating students improving their reading skills to their grade level or above since the Center started in 1993.

In addition to the nonprofits, there are a number of private for-profit companies that provide individual tutorial help. Perhaps the best known of these is the Sylvan Learning Center. Another little known but expanding company that has been very successful in teaching inner city children to read is The Institute for Reading Development (IRD). Although for-profit companies are not viewed favorably by many educators, they can provide a significant force in helping public schools achieve their primary mission. The job of school districts is to increase student achievement. As such, it should make little difference how a district gets that accomplished. If a private for-profit company gets positive results at a cost that is equal to, or lower than, what the school/district can provide, then nothing should prevent the school/district from contracting with that private for-profit company. The fact that we should keep in mind is not whether an organization is non-profit or for-profit but that we get the mission accomplished.

One of the biggest hurdles to tutorial programs is funding. Once again, there are a number of sources of funds that can be tapped. Many schools/districts that are eligible use Title I funds to provide tutoring programs. Regardless of the funding source, tutoring is one of the best ways to increase student achievement and should be available in every school.

Focus the Curriculum

Use a Standards-Based Approach

One of the trends that swept the country in the late 1990s and continues in the early 2000s is standards-based education. Is this approach justifiable? Will this trend last, or will it, too, become a fad that is with education for a short while and then disappears as another fad takes its place? Does standards-based education emphasize academic achievement too much and at the expense of other equally worthwhile goals? What are the results in those states that have used standards-based education for a number of years?

Before those questions can really be answered, an operating definition of standards-based education needs to be provided. Standards are those things that students should know and should be able to do. Standards-based education, then, is nothing more than identifying those elements or skills of the curriculum that are to be taught and then determining to what extent all students will be expected to master them (setting the standards). To do this, an assessment of some type must be identified or designed and then administered at specified grade levels to determine if students are learning at the predetermined acceptable levels. In most states or localities using standards-based education, the basic skills of reading, writing, and mathematics are the first, and sometimes the only, elements or skills that are contained in a standards program. More and more states are now adopting a few other standards areas, especially science.

The specifics of each program are a little different. In some states, all children are assessed, even if it is obvious that some students cannot meet the proficiency levels. Because public education is expected to educate all children, including those that are handicapped or disabled, there are a number of special-education students who will never be able to write a sentence, let alone an organized coherent response to a writing prompt. Another example is a non-English speaking student who has just arrived in the United States and who has not yet had an opportunity to learn English. In states like Colorado, these students must be included in the assessment where they negatively skew the results of the test. In other states, such children are not expected to be able to be proficient, are excused from the assessment, and are not included in the results.

Some states emphasize the earlier elementary grades for assessment whereas others, such as Florida, test all school levels—this includes a high-stakes high-school assessment that determines if a student is qualified to earn a diploma. Some places still use a variety of assessment devices, but almost all use some sort of criterion-referenced test that measures students against the standards instead of against other students.

In those states that have been in the standards business for some time, the results have routinely been increased academic achievement. Texas is a prime example. Fairly dramatic increases have occurred in Texas, especially in the traditionally difficult-to-improve minority population groups. The disaggregated data in Texas shows that the low-income at-risk population so often linked to race in our country has made dramatic gains in student learning and achievement. Texas has been touted as the model to follow, especially for the disenfranchised. Other states have shown similar, if not quite so dramatic, improvement.

Why have Texas and other places using a standards-based education model been successful? I believe the answer is very simple. It has focused everyone's attention on what they are expected to do. No one can escape a standards-based approach. It goes right to the very core of improvement, and that is the classroom and the things that are taught in that classroom. Everyone knows at least the general standards for which they are accountable. A teacher's favorite unit that does not correspond to the standards now must be thrown out or modified so that it does teach to the standards. New units are developed that specifically target the standards. From a school and district-level perspective, the old scope and sequence must be examined and changed to give teachers a more detailed guide on how to reach the more globally-stated standard. School boards now know what to expect of schools. In short, everyone is more focused than they were before standards.

What about those who worry that standards-based education is really a return to the "basics" and that the real job of education is being lost? Those who express such fears seem to be afraid that the other attributes that education brings to children will somehow be lost. As is described in Chapter 1, dealing with a limited mission statement, I do not believe that this is the case. To focus on the primary job of education is not to eliminate the many other facets of education that we find beneficial to children. It merely places those other facets in a supporting, yet vital, role. Standards-based education is not the "dark side of the force" but an approach that focuses our attention on the primary task at hand, and that is student achievement.

Align Vertical Curriculum

A standards-based approach makes it easier to accomplish another critical step that must be in place if student achievement is to increase. The curriculum must be aligned vertically so that teachers at each grade level know what has been introduced to students in the preceding grades and what they are expected to introduce before the students move on to the next grade. The importance of this simple concept cannot be overestimated. Teachers cannot be expected to be curriculum experts who intuitively know what the sequence of instruction should be. Regardless of the quality of the teacher, unless everyone understands what part they play in the whole K–12 curriculum, duplication and gaps occur. Teachers at different grade levels will wind up teaching the same concepts that have already been taught and learned unless vertical alignment of the curriculum occurs. Likewise, unless everyone knows what everyone else is doing, significant gaps in student learning will occur.

Aligning the vertical curriculum leads to the question of whether or not it is preferable for students to be taught a national, state, or local curriculum. We have seen from TIMSS and other similar studies that many countries outside of the United States whose students achieve at high levels are taught a national curriculum used everywhere throughout that country. Again, the argument is that teachers do not need to spend their valuable time developing and aligning curriculum. Instead, they can become experts in the delivery of the instruction. In many ways this makes imminent sense.

A national curriculum makes sense in other ways as well. Perhaps the most compelling is politics. The place where the most effective political pressure can be brought to bear is at the local level. Many times, this pressure has very little if anything to do with student achievement. More often, it is about facets of the educational process that detract from student achievement and drain precious scarce resources away from the core mission of the district. An example will help illustrate the point. In one of the districts in which I worked, we decided to do the unthinkable, i.e., eliminate the Drug and Alcohol Resistance Education (DARE) program. The reason we made the decision was that we felt that the research showed fairly con-clusively that it simply did not work. Indeed, one of the na-tional television networks produced an hour-long special de-tailing that not only did DARE not work, but that for suburban districts like the one in which I worked, DARE actually may increase the use of drugs and alcohol. When the announce-ment was made that the elimination of DARE was being con-sidered, every DARE supporter surfaced and proclaimed the program invaluable despite what the research had found. They gave many anecdotal examples of how it had positively affected them or someone they knew. There is no doubt that DARE is beneficial to many young people and that it has had a positive influence on thousands of adolescents. Nonetheless, it has had no positive effect on reducing drug or alcohol usage for the student population as a whole. People supported DARE because it is a symbol of our failing efforts to prevent young people from using drugs. Even when it was announced that DARE would be replaced by another drug education pro-gram that had been proven to be effective, many people lob-bied to maintain the DARE program. In this particular case, common sense prevailed and the DARE program was re-placed with a program that had proven more effective and less expensive. It may very well be that a national curriculum can be determined in less of a political climate. That does not mean that politics would not be present at the national level. It sim-ply means that decisions can be made away from the glare of television cameras and newspapers and can be made for the right reasons. Researched facts, and not mere opinion, could determine a national curriculum.

A number of other related, but different, reasons justify a national curriculum. Just as a horizontally and vertically aligned curriculum in a local school or district allows a stu-dent to move from grade to grade and school to school within the district without disruption of meaningful instruction, a national curriculum allows students to move from town to town or state to state with an even delivery of what is taught. It allows consistent, coordinated instruction. Statistics bolster the importance of this advantage with an estimated one-fifth of all school age children moving from school to school within a state each year. For high-poverty schools, this number is one-third.

Many schools/districts point to assessment data that reveal that the longer students are educated in their schools/districts, the better they do when compared to students who have not been in the school/district as long. They then interpret this to mean that their school/district does better at educating children than the districts from which the children came. Another reason that is just as plausible, if not more so, is that the students who have been in the school/district longer have had the advantage of an aligned curriculum, whereas those students that have moved from location to location have not.

A national curriculum has other advantages. It provides direction for publishers of textbooks and other instructional materials. It also narrows or focuses staff development within the public school setting as well as providing guidance to college/university teacher training programs. Finally, students get increased time on task because teachers do not need to review previously taught material for the first several weeks of school because they know that all of their students would have learned the same material in the previous years.

Others will argue that state and local control are vital. They argue that people in Washington, D.C., do not know the needs of the children in Texas or Michigan or Vermont or California. Therefore, curriculum control should remain in the hands of the people closest to the children. There is no doubt that a national curriculum would take away some of the control at the local level, but, if a national curriculum works for other countries, perhaps we should give it a try in the United States. However, a school/district really has no control over whether or not we will eventually have a national curriculum. In the interim, schools/districts have much control over the curriculum, including whether or not it is vertically aligned. For increased achievement, such vertical alignment is crucial.

Increase Graduation Requirements

One sure way of increasing student achievement is to increase the graduation requirements in the core academic subject areas. As with many of the other elements that have already been addressed, this sounds easier than it will prove to be. Individuals who mean well will come to the forefront to argue why this is damaging to adolescents and should not be done. But, if a school/district wishes to increase achievement, it should increase graduation requirements.

If we surveyed the general public, we would probably find that most citizens believe that high school is the toughest school level in the K–12 public school system. That makes logical sense. However, that often may not be the case. Indeed, a case can be made that high school is perhaps the academically easiest of all of the school levels when time spent on the core academic subject areas is considered. I did not think this way until I closely examined the requirements that the high schools in the districts in which I have worked had in place. All of these districts took great pride in the quality of their graduates and rightly so. These are quality high schools where most anyone would be proud to enroll their children. However, what I found startled me. In order for students to receive a diploma from these schools, they only needed to complete less than half of their Carnegie course requirements in the core academic subject areas. If a high-school day is approximately six hours long, this means that less than three hours per day was required of a student to study English, mathematics, social studies, science, or foreign language. For the majority of the day, the student was engaged in other coursework or activities.

The *Prisoners of Time* study confirmed my own investigation. The Commission found that in the freshman through senior years, American students spend half as much time in core academic instruction as their counterparts in France, Germany, and Japan. These data are even more compelling when one remembers that the *Prisoners of Time* study included the arts as a part of the core academic day. The statistics are staggering as reflected in the following chart, taken from the report.

The Final Four Years in Four Nations: Estimated Required Core Academic Time

US   ++++++++++++ 1460

Japan   +++++++++++++++++++++++++++++++ 3170

France   ++++++++++++++++++++++++++++++++ 3280

Germany ++++++++++++++++++++++++++++++++++++++3528

| 0 | 1000 | 2000 | 3000 | 4000 |

Total Hours Required

It is little wonder that our students tend to compare more favorably to our foreign competitors in the lower grades but get
progressively worse in comparison as they move through the
grade levels.

It is important to note that it is insufficient to merely increase the number of requirements for graduation. The additional requirements must be in the core academic areas—however the core is defined by the school/district. One example of
how a district increased its requirements over a five-year period is shown in the chart that follows. In this example, 1 credit
is equal to 0.5 Carnegie unit.

Increased Graduation Requirements

Subject Area	Old Requirement	New Requirement
	Core	*Core*
English	6	8
Mathematics	4	6
Science	4	6
Health	1	1
Social Studies	6	6
Core Electives	0	6
Core Total	21	33
	Noncore	*Noncore*
Physical Education	3	3
Arts	0	1
Unrestricted Electives	16	11
Grand Total	40	48

As can be seen from the above chart, one of the ways this district increased its graduation requirements, while still providing an element of choice to students, was to require that a certain number of the electives be taken in "core electives" or the defined core academic areas of English, mathematics, social studies, science, or foreign language.

The overall effect for this district was an increase of 57 percent in the minimum core requirements for graduation. The changes made did not affect most of the students who were already strong academically and who were already taking more than the new minimum number of core courses before the requirements were increased. Instead, the changes most directly affected the average to below-average students. It is precisely those students who needed to have the additional courses required. Otherwise, they naturally gravitated toward those courses that were more attractive to them but that would not provide the type of training and background they would need for their adult lives. Thus, an increase in the core academic graduation requirements will most directly affect the very students who need it the most.

One argument against increasing requirements is that students will become disenchanted and will drop out of high school at even higher rates than is currently the case. I believe that this is a spurious argument. First, I have never seen any data to support such a claim. Second, it is often not the course that is of interest to the student but the teacher and methods used. It is still the job of teachers to motivate their students with methodology that excites and interests them. The good teachers already do this. They link the subject matter to the students' real world. In essence, they make it relevant. They use active learning in their teaching styles. They show the same humor and warmth and caring to their students that we as adults crave. When they do these things, students enjoy the course whether it is English literature or physical education. Third, a diploma that is only a shell of what it should be is not worthy of being awarded anyway. A diploma in and of itself has come to mean very little in this country. It has become so meaningless that what universities or post secondary institutions examine is not whether a student received a diploma but what courses the student took while in high school. Finally, core requirements can and should be modified to meet the needs of the students. For students who are college-bound, an English course in American literature may be appropriate. For students bound for a postsecondary technical program, or directly entering the work force, an English class in reading and writing technical manuals may be more useful and appropriate. It is not necessary for all students to study Shakespeare. However, that does not mean that such students should not be required to master other more appropriate core English courses.

The same type of increased requirements can be applied to schools/districts that have performance criteria as part of the prerequisites for graduation. For example, if a school/district formally requires that a student complete a 25-page research paper with a minimum of 10 resource citations, it can increase the rigor by increasing the toughness of the grading rubric. Whether a school/district uses the traditional Carnegie unit as its base graduation requirement, or whether it uses a performance model, the important thing is that graduation requirements must be increased if achievement is to increase.

Introduce Weighted Grades

If increased graduation requirements improve the achievement of average- to below-average–ability students, what can be done to increase achievement for high-ability students? One easy answer is that you can increase the difficulty of those rewards that motivate high achievers in school—grades and academic recognition. One of the best ways to do this is to implement a weighted grades system whereby courses that are deemed to be more rigorous and more difficult by the school/district receive an extra weight to the letter grade received by the student. Most often this takes the form of a 5-point scale instead of a 4-point scale. Thus, an A would receive a 5, a 4 for a B, a 3 for a C, and so forth, whereas a course not weighted would receive a 4 for an A, a 3 for a B, etc. Many high schools throughout the country already use a weighted grade system and find it to be beneficial.

The logic behind a weighted grade system is simple. In an unweighted grading system, courses that do not require much energy or effort currently receive the same value as courses that are generally perceived as being academically rigorous. For example, an A in physical education counts the same as an A in Advanced Placement (AP) physics. When class rank is determined for university consideration or for the determination of valedictorian and salutatorian, the physical education grade is figured into the calculation exactly like the grade in AP physics. Therefore, there is no additional incentive for bright young people to take more rigorous courses. Indeed, there is a disincentive because a lower grade received in AP physics harms a student's ability to be ranked higher in the class standings or to be honored as the top scholar upon graduation. I have personally observed numerous students who elected to take easier courses particularly during their senior year because of the reasons cited above. This is a disservice to those bright young people who should be encouraged to take more rigorous courses. Anything the school/district can do to remove disincentives and to provide positive reasons for taking harder courses should be done.

The introduction of a weighted grades system may well be met with resistance from those teachers who perceive that their areas of expertise will be slighted. Again, this is only human nature and is to be expected. One method of increasing support for a weighted system is to establish a committee of professionals to determine exactly which courses will be weighted and which will not. Instead of selecting courses based on title or reputation, a rubric can be established against which all courses would be judged. If the course meets the requirements of the rubric, it is weighted. If it does not, it is not weighted. Regardless of the system, a method should be established as to which courses will be weighted.

Introduce Harder Subjects Earlier

Much has been written over the years about expectation. Psychologists have demonstrated for decades that people largely perform to the level expected of them. If students are viewed as capable, bright young people, teachers treat them like gifted children and students perform like competent academicians.

The importance of expectation in education came to the forefront during the effective schools research done in the 1980s. The work of Ronald Edmonds, Larry Lezote, and others established that high-performing schools almost always had high expectations for their students regardless of their socioeconomic background or the number of at-risk factors they possessed. Students who were expected to do poorly did poorly, and those that were expected to do well did well. As early as 1981, Thomas Good discovered that based on expectations, teachers behave differently toward children, which, in turn, affects the performance of those same students. In a report entitled *Effective Schools and Effective Classrooms*, Good found that teachers influence the behavior of students based on their expectation of them by:

- Paying less attention to slow students
- Smiling more and having more eye contact with high achievers
- Calling on slow students less frequently
- Waiting less time for slower students to answer
- Seating slow students farther away, thereby providing less monitoring by the teacher
- Criticizing more frequently the incorrect answers of slower students
- Giving slow students less feedback
- Interrupting slower students more frequently
- Requiring less effort and work from slower students
- Praising slower students less often for correct or marginal responses

The call for high expectations has become a mantra in public education. The problem is that the mantra has become almost meaningless because it is so seldom translated into practical steps that a school/district can take to actually demonstrate higher expectations. It too often has been left to the individual classroom teacher to determine the appropriate expectation level for individual students as well as the entire group. When coupled with the traditional scope and sequence guides that have been used for the last several decades, this has resulted in information, topics, or subjects not being introduced to students because of a belief that the students were not ready to learn such material.

The 1995 TIMSS report confirms, and the 1999 TIMSS report reaffirms, that American students fail to encounter more difficult material at as early an age as do the students in the other nations participating in the TIMSS study. Specifically, they found that the TIMSS assessment covered content that is introduced later in the United States curriculum than it is introduced on average in the other TIMSS countries. The content of the mathematics assessment was most equivalent to curriculum introduced in the ninth grade in the United States but the seventh grade in the other TIMSS countries. Likewise, the content of the science curriculum was most equivalent to the eleventh grade in America but the ninth grade in the rest of the TIMSS countries. The TIMSS report found that this difference reflects the traditional late appearance of algebra and geometry in the mathematics area, and chemistry and physics in the science curriculum.

This finding is also consistent with the actions and recommendations made by The College Board through their STEP-UP Program. They found that certain courses could be considered as "gate keeper" courses for students who eventually entered college. These courses are algebra and geometry. They found that far fewer minorities take these courses, and that minority students who fail to take these courses rarely go on to enter and graduate from college, even though they have the innate ability to successfully complete the courses and to become a college graduate. This was verified by a study conducted by the Education Trust in 1997. This study found that of every 100 high-scoring white students in a California school district, 88 took algebra. For every 100 Asians, 100 were admitted into algebra. However, for every 100 black students the number taking algebra was 51, and for every 100 Latinos, only 42 enrolled. It appears from TIMSS, The College Board, and the Education Trust that these courses are extremely important for our young people today and for the United States as a whole.

The majority of other industrialized countries introduce algebra, geometry, chemistry, and physics two years prior to the U.S. Should we have the same level of expectation as these countries or should we continue the traditional scope and sequence we have used in the United States for the last 50 years? The data dictates that if a school/district desires to increase student achievement it should shift to the earlier introduction of these courses in our curriculum.

In a number of our more affluent suburbs in the U.S., the schools/districts have already introduced algebra and geometry in middle school. This is commendable. For many of these districts, comparisons of their students' achievement to the countries that participated in the TIMSS assessment should be favorable and, indeed, that is what occurred. The districts of this nature that did actually participate in the 1995 and 1999 TIMSS studies performed well and ranked near the top of all TIMSS participants. The only local districts that participated in the 1995 TIMSS were a group of districts near Chicago that labeled themselves The First in the World Consortium. When compared to all of the TIMSS countries, this consortium ranked second in mathematics, behind only Singapore. They were not statistically different from six countries but were statistically better than 34 others. The consortium did even better in science, where it was ranked first. The consortium was not statistically different from eight countries but was statistically better than 33 others. While this group of eighth graders was from a select group of school districts in the country, they still demonstrate that if schools/districts have high expectations and introduce harder courses earlier, the United States can compete on an equal footing with K–12 schools/systems anywhere in the world.

Similar results occurred in the 1999 TIMSS. A number of groups of school districts that introduce harder mathematics and science subjects earlier performed at or near the top of all TIMSS participants. The top three such district groups and their final ranking for both mathematics and science are listed below.

Top Three United States Local School Districts Based on World Ranking on 1999 TIMSS

District	Mathematics Ranking	Science Ranking
First in the World Consortium (IL)	8	4
Michigan Invitational Group	9	5
Naperville (IL) School District #203	6	1

Although mathematics and science are the prime examples of subjects that should be moved to an earlier spot in the curriculum, other subjects are also appropriate for such acceleration. Foreign language is a perfect example. I believe a clear consensus of Americans, if polled, would no doubt agree that we can do a better job of teaching foreign language. Unlike most European and Asian countries, we wait until the high-school years to teach a foreign language. We introduce foreign language in the middle-school years. Because middle-school philosophy espouses experimentation in early adolescence, little is accomplished in most middle-school foreign language classes other than an overview of foreign cultures that use a particular language. Although this is a worthwhile goal, it is not the teaching of a foreign language.

We know that children's speech and dialect patterns have long been established before adolescence. This makes it extremely difficult for American students who do not start learning another language until approximately 15 years of age to properly speak and understand another language. Europeans, on the other hand, routinely learn a second and third language when they are young. It is not hard to understand that if we wish our students to learn a foreign language we need to start early, as early as kindergarten, and not wait until high school.

A handful of schools/districts across the country have demonstrated that when a second language is introduced in the elementary grades, our students can be just as fluent and conversant in other languages as European children. In summary, whether it is algebra, geometry, chemistry, physics, foreign language, or other content areas, if a school/district wishes to increase student achievement, it must teach harder content areas earlier.

Prevent Regression to Easier Subjects

Anyone who has ever worked on a high school campus is familiar with "senioritis." This malady strikes many young people during the last year of their K–12 public school career. In many schools/districts, seniors have often completed virtually all of the requirements for graduation. They view themselves as adults and are often not motivated to work hard during their last year in the K–12 system. They believe they have worked hard during the previous 12 years and they deserve to have a more relaxed year. The end result is often a selection of courses that often does not challenge the student. Indeed, many students do not even take a full load of courses but, instead, leave campus early for part-time jobs or to simply hang out. Whether it is a reduction in course load or the enrollment in classes that will not challenge the student, it needs to be prevented. A simple but effective way to prevent such regression is to prohibit high-school students from taking courses that are easier than ones they have already completed or from taking anything but a full load of academic subjects.

Students will often avoid a hard senior year by electing to take courses in the noncore academic areas. It bears repeating that such courses have a very valid place in the school/district curriculum and students should be encouraged to take such courses to be a well-rounded person. However, an overenrollment in such courses in the senior or any other year is to be avoided if academic achievement is to be enhanced. If a school/district has rigorous graduation requirements in place, a full senior year would naturally result, or the student would fail to meet the requirements for graduation. Without such rigorous requirements, a separate policy regarding this issue would be required.

The areas where students most often regress to subjects that are easier are mathematics and science. It is a tragedy when a capable student who has completed trigonometry decides to take a sophomore geography class instead of a senior calculus course. It is equally tragic when a student who has completed an AP chemistry class decides to take a practical physics class instead of the more rigorous theoretical AP physics course. A school/district policy needs to be developed that prohibits such regression from occurring unless it is determined by the school counselor or administrator that it is in the best interest of the student to do so. This would force a discussion of the issue with the student with a default position that unless a valid reason could be provided as to why an exception should be made, the student would be required to take the more rigorous course of study.

As with most of the steps needed to increase academic achievement, there will be people who will object to such a policy. Some students will protest and many will be joined by their parents. However, the school/district needs to stand by such a policy and insist that a rigorous curriculum be followed unless there are obvious reasons why such a policy is detrimental to a particular student. To be fair to students, such a policy would need to be phased in over a period of four years. This would allow the school/district officials to communicate the policy with every student who enrolls in the school, thus preventing a possible confrontation three years later when the student is entering the senior year.

Eliminate Grade Inflation

When one reviews the literature regarding grade inflation in the K–12 public schools, no firm conclusion can be reached as to whether grade inflation, in fact, exists or whether or not this often publicized phenomenon is another commonly held, but baseless, belief of the general public. There seems to be little question that grade inflation exists in the colleges and universities of this country. This postsecondary problem rears its ugly head every so often, with the latest revelation of the problem coming April 19, 2002, when the Associated Press released a story from one of, if not the most, prestigious universities in the world—Harvard. According to the news release, which was based on a study conducted by Harvard itself, 91 percent of the university's June 2001 senior class graduated with some kind of honor on their diploma and almost half of all undergraduate grades for the same academic year were A or A-minus. The university president, Dr. Lawrence H. Summers, denounced such grade inflation and vowed that the famous institution would take steps to alter the situation, including limiting the honors designation to a maximum of 60 percent of graduates. This is more consistent with other Ivy League schools such as Princeton and Yale, which limit total honors to approximately one-third of the graduating class.

Further evidence of post-secondary grade inflation comes from a report on Ivy League schools by the American Academy of Arts and Sciences. It showed that the number of Harvard undergraduate students who received A's rose from 22 percent in 1966 to 46 percent 30 years later in 1996 and that the percentage of A's received by Princeton students rose from 31 percent in 1973 to 43 percent in 1997. One other amazing statistic from the study revealed that only 12 percent of all grades received at Princeton in 1997 were a C or lower and that fewer than 20 percent of all university students in the United States received grades less than a B-minus. This statistic is startling when one considers that in the same year approximately 32 percent of all entering college freshmen had to take at least one remedial course.

However, no such clear cut evidence seems to exist for K–12 public schools. Rather, there seems to be conflicting reports as to the existence of grade inflation, or if it exists at all, the severity of the inflation. For example, after analyzing data for almost 24,000 high school students, Daniel Koretz and Mark Berends, working for the Rand Corporation, concluded in a study entitled, *Changes in High School Grading Standards in Mathematics 1982–1992*, that there was "no large-scale, substantial grade inflation, at least in mathematics, between 1982 and 1992." Their findings were as follows:

Average GPA for 1982 and 1992 High School Students

	1982		1992	
Course	*Students*	*GPA*	*Students*	*GPA*
Total	12,324	2.20	11,522	2.23
Algebra I	7,906	2.24	8,104	2.21
Algebra II	5,596	2.38	7,765	2.28
Advanced	1,332	2.70	2,113	2.70

As can be seen from the chart, GPA actually stayed the same or declined in all of the more difficult mathematics courses. Certainly, this report supports the belief that there would seem to be no grade inflation in K–12 public education.

Unconfirmed reports in the popular media have indicated that senior research analysts with the United States Department of Education have concluded that there is simply no way to accurately determine if grade inflation has occurred or not.

A couple of conflicting reports comes from the two main entrance examinations used by colleges and universities throughout the United States, i.e., the SAT and the ACT. The report for the 2001 ACT results reveals a gradual but continuing trend to rising GPA's. The following chart shows this trend.

Average Reported GPA (4.0 Scale) Among ACT-Tested High-School Graduates: 1996–2001

	Year					
	1996	*1997*	*1998*	*1999*	*2000*	*2001*
GPA	3.14	3.16	3.17	3.19	3.20	3.22

The SAT reveals a similar but even more dramatic inflation. From 1984 to 1999, the percentage of students taking the SAT who reported an A average increased from 28 percent to 39 percent for an 11 percent increase over the 15-year period. This increase came despite no demonstrable improvement in SAT scores during that same period.

It seems that one can make a case for or against the actual presence of grade inflation in our K–12 public schools. One fact appears to come through the research, regardless of whether the conclusions drawn from the research are that there is or is not grade inflation, and that is that students from high-income families and those from inner-city urban schools seem to receive higher grades. This was found in the Koretz and Berends study and in a report entitled *National Education Longitudinal Study of 1988*. The NELS study showed that a large percentage of students in both low-poverty and high-poverty schools get A's but their respective achievement is widely disparate when measured by the scores of 8th graders on the NELS. In addition, in a report by the United States Department of Education, students in high-poverty schools who got A's in English scored approximately the same on the reading section of the SAT as students in affluent schools who received C's or D's. Judith Anderson, research analyst with the

Office of Educational Research and Improvement with the United States Department of Education found that the differences between grades and high scores on the mathematics portion of the SAT was even greater. The high-poverty school students who received A's scored about the same as those students from affluent schools who received D's.

There are many educators who argue that the grades a student receives are not really important. In addition, many reports indicate that teachers and schools use grades for many different reasons, only one of which is to accurately report on the actual performance of the student in learning the material. Teachers may use grades to motivate students to try harder or to reward students who worked hard but still struggled with the material. Obviously, there are many different possible purposes of grades for individual students, and they all probably have a place. However, the purpose of this section of the book is not to debate what the purpose of grades should be as they apply to individual students. Regardless of the purpose of grades for individuals, I believe that the research supports the idea that achievement can be harmed if grades are used in such a way that widespread grade inflation results. There should be a clear link between grades for a student body as a whole and the performance those same students obtain on objective achievement measures. This is of particular importance to high-poverty schools and districts. If the research is correct regarding elevated grades and low achievement on such measures as the SAT for students in high-poverty schools, it is especially important for such schools and districts to eliminate grade inflation. There are a number of different ways that such grade inflation can be controlled and the exact method to be used should be left to the discretion of the individual school. Obviously, this is not a matter that can be left to the individual teacher. The faculty as a whole must determine how to eliminate grade inflation and then put into practice the method they have selected. Only by acting as one unit can the result be grades that are linked to actual achievement. As a result, there should be a commensurate rise in achievement.

Teach What Is Tested and
Test What is Taught

For many years educators and the lay public alike have argued over whether it is wise to teach to the test or to ignore the assessment and teach the curriculum regardless of whether or not it contains the specific type of material contained in the assessment. For those of us who have long believed that it makes absolutely no sense to test material that is not taught, the recent shift to standards-based education and the criterion-referenced assessments that accompany this movement is a welcome reinforcement for our position. It is a shift to common sense and it makes no difference whether the test is a standards-based one or a standardized one. The only logical approach to assessment and learning is that you test what you teach and that you teach what you test.

Critics of public education often decry the logic of teaching to the test. They argue that it is a way for public education to appear to get better results than is actually the case. One usually sees this argument when an increase in test scores is reported. Because critics of public education do not believe that public educators can get increased achievement, they reason that something must be wrong with the assessment. They would argue that one of three things happened: (a) the test got easier, (b) the grading of the test got easier, or (c) someone manipulated the statistics to make it appear that students did better. When these excuses are nullified, the critics jump on the fact that people were teaching to the test. Of course teaching to the test is much different from teaching *the* test. As Nancy Grasmick, the state superintendent of schools for Maryland, asserted when trying to defend the alignment of Maryland's state assessment to the state's newly adopted standards, "If you're teaching to the test and you're mirroring good teaching that will enhance learning, then we don't see anything wrong with that."

An example will iterate the logic of teaching to the test. The example is common to all places in the United States and most of the world. To secure a driver's license, a person must take both a paper-and-pencil type test and an actual driving performance test. For the written portion, people are given a booklet by the state highway patrol that contains all of the things they want people to know before they get behind a wheel to drive. The booklet contains the speed limits, the various traffic signs and what they mean, the stopping distance required for different speeds, and various other content knowledge. The state then administers the examination to determine if people know the material. In other words, they give people exactly the material they need to learn to be permitted to drive and then they test them to see if they learned it. If people fail the test, they must study the material some more and retake the test until they have mastered the material. The state patrol does not omit from the brochure some of the material they believe is important for you to learn and then test you to see if you somehow learned the omitted material from some other source. They also do not include information in the booklet that is not relevant to driving safely and require one to learn it even though it will never be included in an assessment. If either of these two things occurred, people would become angry because it simply would not make sense. School should be no different.

The need to align the curriculum to the test received a big boost in the early nineties from Fenwick English of the University of Cincinnati and now at the Unitversity of North Carolina. English designed the concept of a curriculum audit for schools/districts. Although a curriculum audit contained many facets, the primary driving force behind the audit was the determination of whether the school's/district's policies aligned with the stated or written curriculum; if the materials and textbooks used were aligned with the written curriculum; if the written curriculum was aligned to the taught curriculum (what was actually taught by teachers in the classroom); and if everything was aligned with what the tests actually assessed. Any school/district that wants to increase student achievement can make giant strides by aligning the assessments to the curriculum or the curriculum to the assessments. It will not guarantee that achievement will rise, but it will go a long way to removing a barrier that will almost assuredly guarantee that you will not increase achievement.

Obvious misalignments can occur in even the best of schools/districts. A personal example will illustrate. Upon entering a district as its superintendent, one of the first things that I did was look for obvious misalignments. It is often easier to spot such misalignments at the secondary level where subject-area courses are normally taught at specific grade levels. In this case, the misalignment was with the year that American History was being taught and the year that the Iowa Test of Educational Development (ITED) was administered. The ITED contains sections in the social studies subtest that relate directly to American History. Therefore, it is important to teach American History before the ITED is taken at the high-school level. In this case, American History was being taught in the junior year and the ITED was being administered during the sophomore year. Naturally, the results of the social studies subtest were deflated and were not reflective of the material that students learned before they graduated from high school. Clearly, a change was in order and was put into place. The result was an increase of five percentile in student norms in the following year in the social studies portion of the ITED. This increase was sustained the following year. In this example, what or how much students learned by the time they graduated was not changed, but the results that were reported to the public to reveal how well or how poorly schools/districts were doing, did increase.

In conclusion, teaching to the test should no longer be a debatable practice. For schools/districts that wish to increase student achievement, the only reasonable approach is to teach what is to be tested and to test what was taught. To do otherwise is to cheat our students.

Modify Practices That
Lower Student Achievement

Before one begins to read the next section of this book, a few introductory statements need to be made. First, the author is a lifelong educator with well over 30 years of experience in a variety of different educational environments, including work at the local, regional, state and university levels and in a variety of administrative positions. In short, I am probably as much of an educator as anyone reading this book. As such, though I may not deserve the same credit as most educators receive for the many good things that routinely happen every day in education, I certainly deserve the same criticisms as any other educator for the failures that the profession sometimes makes. Thus, the criticisms that follow are as much a criticism of myself as they are of other educators. Criticism is not something that we as human beings relish. The best of us accept constructive criticism for how it is intended, i.e., to improve a current situation and to make it better. Consequently, I offer the following criticisms with the best of intentions.

Second, professions are like individual human beings. They have strengths and weaknesses and they have their own idiosyncrasies that make them unique relative to other professions. Professional educators must look at the strengths and weaknesses that the profession possesses as well as exploring how the weaknesses develop. In short, educators must be willing to objectively examine whether the commonly-held educational beliefs are based on fact and, if they are not, to change them. As such, the author presents the following ideas that run directly counter to what many, if not most, educators profess to believe. The intent is not to cast blame, but to recognize that certain educational practices that lower student achievement are commonplace throughout the country.

Much criticism has been leveled at education for being too willing to embrace new programs without first closely examining the effects such programs have on student achievement. What appears to be a good idea often becomes the latest fad and quickly spreads throughout the country. As the idea spreads, the program, which may have originally had a sound basis, becomes altered, often to the point that it is no longer recognizable except in name only. Soon it becomes almost impossible for the vast majority of educators to resist or stop the impetus of the new program from catching hold in their own school/district. Some of these practices often become so ingrained and so well established that they last for a very long time, and, during that entire time, student achievement declines or fails to be what it can and should be.

It is important to note that new ideas and new programs are essential if we are to improve student learning. We know much more today about how to teach students than we have ever known before. We must continue to search out methods of improving student learning and achievement. It is, therefore, important not to fall into the trap of avoiding all new ideas or programs as fads that have no validity. We cannot continue to teach the same way that we have been teaching for the last 100 years. Instead, we must carefully examine new program ideas and test their validity before jumping on the most current bandwagon. Likewise, we must examine some of the more recent programs, ideas and philosophies to determine if they have had a positive or negative influence on student achievement. Invariably, there will be some that have been detrimental to achievement. These must be identified and then eliminated or modified. In short, we must drive out harmful practices. The following are those that I believe need to be closely scrutinized.

Whole Language

The "whole language" approach is perhaps the epitome of a good approach gone wrong. Originally from New Zealand, which has one of the highest literacy rates in the world, the whole-language method of reading instruction was based on sound principles and an impressive record of success. The method sounds simple enough. It teaches literacy by using a variety of approaches to teach reading skills to children, including providing what educators have come to call a "rich print environment." Students are encouraged to browse through and to use a wide range of printed material. All of the components of language arts are incorporated into the teaching of reading. Thus, reading instruction is done as it naturally occurs to children instead of through artificial time blocks broken up into reading, writing, spelling, speaking, and listening. Of vital importance are the interests of the children, which is why there must be a plethora of print materials. In the early stages, when the concepts of the whole-language approach had not yet been modified through a lengthy adaptation process, the method worked well for most children. Indeed, even today the method works well for a large number of children, especially those who come from rich-print-environment homes during the first five years of their lives. However, through the adaptation process, a number of very important and detrimental changes occurred.

The whole-language approach became viewed as "the" way to teach language arts. As such, it pushed out the old traditional approaches. Out went Spot and Jane, and in came Champion and Javier. The basic readers became viewed as boring (which they were) and therefore detrimental. The result was that no basic reading text or basal was used at all. The entire reading program was left in the hands of the individual teacher. For many teachers, this approach was fun, innovative, and exciting. For the veteran teacher, who had many years of experience with basals, the change to the whole-language approach was smooth. Their experience guided them in knowing what needed to be included in their instruction. They knew what skills students at their grade level had typically learned in the past; consequently, they included those skills in their lesson planning. For beginning teachers, or teachers who were already weak in language arts instruction, the approach proved disastrous. Suddenly, whole groups of children were not being taught the specific skills that many needed to learn to read. The brighter students were able to learn these skills through this more natural approach, but the average to below-average student suffered. They needed specific instruction in specific skills to be successful. Even the bright students were missing critical direct-skill instruction that would make them better readers, writers, speakers, and listeners.

So, the first mistake was in removing the basal reader from the classroom. This does not mean that teachers should be a slave to a basal. They should not be. However, if the basal has been properly written and used in conjunction with ongoing assessment of individual students, it provides an anchor that helps assure that the critical skills necessary for successful reading are taught to all children. This is especially true for beginning or less experienced teachers or those who receive inadequate instruction in how to teach reading in their college education program. In addition, the basals have changed dra-

matically over the last decade. Many now include all of the
components of the rich print environment, including antholo-
gies, which many people found so compelling about the
whole-language approach. The modern basal does not contain
the famous "See Spot Run" with the controlled vocabulary of
the old traditional basal series.

An example of how effective the introduction of a basal
reader can be when used with other approaches by capable
teachers came from a principal, Gloria Steed, who worked in a
district where I was superintendent. Gloria's school selected
the Houghton-Mifflin *Invitations to Literacy* program. In one
year, her school's reading achievement shot up, with the result being that 97 percent of her students scored "proficient"
or better on a state-administered standards-based/criterion-
referenced assessment. This was the fourth highest scoring
school in the entire state. There is no doubt that Gloria's students for that year were talented young people. There is also
no doubt that a number of other very important factors helped
fuel the increase in achievement. There is also no doubt that
the replication of such lofty heights will be difficult to achieve
every year. But just as these things no doubt contributed to the
success of Gloria's school, there is also no doubt that the success experienced in the first year will be continued at some
level in future years and that a basal reader approach will assist in that success.

A second even more critical mistake in the whole-language
movement was the elimination of phonics or phonemic awareness from language arts instruction. Phonics became viewed
as harmful to students. It was viewed as an artificial way of
teaching reading. It was viewed as boring (which it was). It
was believed that children would learn the letter–sound connection in the more natural way. In truth, the whole-language
approach from New Zealand never eliminated phonics instruction from the many approaches used to teach reading.
The original approach understood that, for most children,
phonics is a critical piece of the reading puzzle. For some children, it is *the* critical piece. Without it, they cannot learn to
read. A principal friend of mine, Jim Mahoney, often explained as follows to parents who inquired about phonetic instruc-

tion: "Whole language is a wonderful approach to teach reading but children still need to be taught that the letter B is pronounced 'bu'." Jim has always insisted that his teachers include phonetic instruction for all children, including the best and brightest. This includes the children who attend his current school, which became the first public school in the United States to be approved by the Primary Years International Baccalaureate Program.

A large number of people now recognize the importance of maintaining all of the elements of reading instruction, including phonics. For example, The National Research Council released a study, *Preventing Reading Difficulties in Young Children*, in March 1998 in which it synthesized decades of reading research. It concluded that children learn best when taught to sound out words or through a phonetic approach. They also concluded that children also need creative activities to motivate their interest in reading, which is a cornerstone of the whole-language approach. Catherine Snow, Professor of Education at Harvard University Graduate School of Education concurs. She asserts that because reading is a complex and multifaceted endeavor, no one method is the answer and that children need all of the approaches research indicates are effective.

The third detrimental adaptation of whole language was the degradation of grammar mechanics and spelling rules. Although the creators of whole language never intended this result, the new users of whole language interpreted the approach as being antithetical to these important language arts skills. Today, it is a virtual universal truth that students in the public schools of this country do not know, and are not taught, the rules that help guide a child to learn to spell words correctly. Instead, rote memory is used almost exclusively. Spell-check programs on our computers have added to the lowering of importance that many educators place on spelling in general and on spelling rules in particular. When these rules are taught in conjunction with the other language arts skills, including phonics, achievement increases dramatically. Another principal colleague, Brian Ewert, introduced the *Spelling and Reading with Riggs* model developed by Myrna McCulloch into his school. This approach is an extension of *The Writing Road to Reading* program developed by Romalda Spalding and is often referred to as "The Spalding Method." Achievement in Brian's school rose on the state-administered criterion-referenced examination by double digits in one year. This was in a school that was already scoring well above the state average.

In today's classroom, spelling words most often come from words used in the students' own writings and not from universal spelling lists. This approach does make sense. If a student is already using a word and spells it incorrectly, the word should be targeted for correct spelling. However, unless the child has been taught and has learned the grammar, spelling, and punctuation conventions, the only way he can learn the correct spelling is by rote memory. Even if a teacher does not wish to teach the spelling rules in isolation, the correct spelling of the words students use in their writing can be taught in conjunction with the proper rules.

If a school/district wishes to improve student achievement in language arts, it needs to analyze if a whole-language approach is being used and, if so, if it resembles what the originators intended or if it has become altered. Specifically, the school/district must assure that a quality basal reader, phonics, and grammar/spelling rules are part of the direct instruction. To do otherwise is to leave a large number of children without the basic skills they need in the critical language arts area.

Developmentalism

A second classic example of sound educational pedagogy that turned into a practice that is detrimental to student achievement is the concept of developmentalism. The idea is fundamentally sound. Children are ready to learn material at a given point in time and the introduction of that material sooner will have no positive effect. It is further reasoned that introduction of material too soon could frustrate the child and actually damage the ability for the child to learn the material when they are ready—thus the term *developmentalism*.

The concept goes further. Different children learn at different rates. What one child can learn at age two, another child may not be ready to learn until age three. Both children are perfectly normal. They simply learn different material at different rates. Eric Jensen confirms this in the case of reading. His studies indicate that children may differ in their readiness to learn to read by as much as three years. Once again, we know this to be the case. Children do learn at different rates. When one child is developmentally ready, another is not.

Finally, many developmentalists assert that a child needs certain prerequisite learnings before she is ready to learn more advanced material or skills. These are often referred to as prereadiness activities. Once again, this is based on sound research that also makes intuitive sense. A child who has not been read to, allowed to manipulate and handle books, or who has not had the chance to draw and color, will not be ready to begin to learn the shapes and sounds of letters.

Educators who classify themselves as developmentalists dominate the early childhood grades in many, if not most, of our public schools/districts. They are very ardent about when material should, and should not, be introduced into the curriculum. Usually, the controversy comes at kindergarten. Many developmentalists argue that five-year-old children are not developmentally ready to learn to read. Instead, they engage students in prereadiness activities and slowly introduce letter recognition. There are two problems associated with this practice. The first is that because different children are developmentally ready at different times, some of the students on the first day of kindergarten are either ready to begin learning letter recognition, or are, in fact, already reading. For these children, the prereadiness activities in which many kindergarten teachers insist that all children engage are unnecessary and boring. For these children, waiting to learn material for which they are ready is detrimental. In fact, some children may hide their ability to read so as not to stand out as unusual. It is just as detrimental for these children not to be provided the opportunity to move forward with their learning as it is for those who are not ready to have material introduced too soon. The net effect is that student learning and achievement for the group as a whole is lowered. It is for this reason that the public schools lose many bright children to private institutions, which tend to teach children to their individual, developmentally appropriate level. Of course, many parents cannot afford a private school alternative, nor are they provided a public school choice alternative.

The second problem with the insistence that all children participate in kindergarten prereadiness activities is even greater than the first. The assumption is that five-year-old children are not ready to read and, therefore, they are not expected to be able to do so. This expectation level is simply too low. Expectation drives achievement. If a teacher does not believe that children can actually be reading by the end of kindergarten, then they will not be. If the teacher believes and expects her students to read by the end of kindergarten, then most likely they will.

These statements are, of course, gross simplifications. There are children who will not be able to learn to read by the end of kindergarten. The point is that American public education holds the belief that kindergarten children cannot be expected to learn to read. Therefore, the job of the kindergarten teacher has become one of preparing children through the use of numerous prereadiness materials and activities to learn to read in the first grade. If this were, in fact true, then it would follow that children all over the world would also not be able to learn to read in kindergarten. However, this is not the case. Children in a number of other countries routinely learn to read in kindergarten. France is a good example where virtually all children leave kindergarten knowing how to read. Many French children have the further advantage of having formal preschool experiences at the ages of three to four, but if French children can learn to read in kindergarten, so can American children. The simple truth is that we hold our expectations too low, and this must be changed.

The National Research Council in its aforementioned report, *Preventing Reading Difficulties in Young Children* shares the belief that children can learn to read at earlier levels. The study reports that the research shows that by focusing on the basic reading skills, starting in preschool, most reading problems can be prevented. They revealed that those children who have successfully learned to read by the time they enter elementary school have mastered three main skills. These are: (a) they understand that the letters of the alphabet represent sounds; (b) they are able to read for meaning; and (c) they read fluently. They maintain that children who have difficulty in learning to read simply need more focused, intense, and individual teaching methods. The report contends that there is a need for more preschool program experiences that teach children such things as breaking words into syllable sounds or rhyming.

Regardless of the developmentalists, a growing number of people feel that it is critical to focus on reading and mathematics, especially in the early grades. Bill Honig, the former state superintendent of public instruction in California expressed it this way: "Kindergarten and first grade should be about getting basic reading and math. If you can't do that, everything else starts to disintegrate." The growing number of people who believe that learning to read early is critical to later school success is based on a growing amount of research. Some of this has been reported in *The 90 percent Reading Goal* published by Lynn Fielding, Nancy Kerr, and Paul Rosier. They write on the research of Torgesen, Juel, and Francis and report the following:

Children Seldom Catch Up

More than eight of ten children with severe word reading problems at the end of the first grade performed below the average range at the beginning of the third grade.

Children who fall behind in the first grade have a one in eight chance of ever catching up to grade level without extraordinary efforts.

Eighty-eight percent of children who were deficient in word recognition skills in the first grade were poor readers in fourth grade.

Seventy-four percent of children who are poor readers in the third grade remain poor readers in the ninth grade.

The statistics from these research efforts are truly remarkable and clearly point to the need to alter our perceptions of what children can and must learn in the early childhood years. If we fail them in kindergarten and first grade, we most likely doom them to years of frustration and failure.

Finally, some of the recent brain research reinforces the need to change the current thinking of what developmentalism means. There is evidence that a child has a window of opportunity to learn certain information. Although that window may vary in width depending on the child and the material, the window does not remain open indefinitely. If not learned within that window of opportunity, the material may never be learned, or may be harder to learn. Learning to play a musical instrument or learning a foreign language are good examples of this window of opportunity. It becomes critical, therefore, that true reading and mathematics instruction begin for children when they are ready—and that is often in kindergarten.

Lessening of Importance of Basic Mathematical Computation

A debate has occurred over the last few years as to the advisability of students using calculators. Most educators probably fall on the side of the debate that allows the use of calculators, whereas many parents do not. I fall on the side of most educators. The fear seems to be that students will not adequately learn basic mathematics computation if they are allowed to rely upon calculators. Educators argue that to deny calculators for student use is illogical because they are so prevalent in the real world. The real question, however, is not whether students should be allowed to use calculators but whether students should be required to learn basic computation.

According to the National Assessment of Educational Progress (NAEP), students today are performing about the same as they were 17 years ago. Unfortunately, we have not increased students' abilities to learn basic mathematics computation. As Richard Colvin has pointed out in an article he wrote for *The School Administrator*, only about 60 percent of high-school seniors can compute with decimals, fractions, and percentages, whereas fewer than 10 percent can use beginning algebra. He also points to the university system in California, where 54 percent of entering freshmen must take remedial mathematics courses, as an example of how poorly even our high-school graduates are doing in the area of mathematical computation.

Fortunately, many individuals and groups have seen the damage and are calling for a balance. For example, the National Council of Teachers of Mathematics (NCTM) is joining this call for more balance in its reformulated standards. According to Glenda Lappan, a former president of NCTM and a professor at Michigan State University, one of the objects of the new standards appears to be for students to develop a deeper understanding of basic algorithms, including their proficiency and ease in using them.

The results of a de-emphasis on computational skills can be readily seen in most any school/district. It is commonplace to see fourth and fifth graders still using their fingers to perform computations of the simplest nature. This should not be the case. There are a number of mathematics computation facts that must be memorized, and memorized so well that they can be recalled at any time in a quick—indeed an automatic—fashion. This may seem boring to the students, and it may cause the teacher and parent a headache, but it must be done. To memorize such facts, it also takes boring practice to ensure that the proper brain patterns are established enabling the memorized facts to go into long-term memory. It also means that these facts must be recalled and practiced periodically to reinforce the long-term memory brain patterns. There are any number of ways, many of which are fun and motivating, that such facts can be taught in the classroom. The important point is that the school/district makes sure that the curriculum contains these skills and that they are, in fact, being taught in the classroom. Once the facts have been learned, then students can use calculators as they use computation in a normal, real-world manner to solve much more complex problems.

Multiple Intelligences

Another example of research that has been transmuted into educational practices that are not producing increased achievement is Howard Gardner's work on multiple intelligences. Gardner, a researcher and theorist from Harvard University, who never dreamed that the education community would so readily adopt his work, departs from the traditional view of intelligence being narrowly confined to the linguistic/language and logical/mathematical areas. His view is both intriguing and probably correct. His original seven intelligences, and the recently added eighth, are:

1. Spatial
2. Kinesthetic
3. Musical
4 Linguistic
5. Logical/mathematical
6. Interpersonal
7. Intrapersonal
8. Naturalist

My contention is that in most instances, schools/districts that focus on multiple intelligences are doomed to lower achievement. There are a number of reasons for this, none of which has to do with the validity of Gardner's theory. First, one must carefully examine the underlying and probably unconscious reasons why a school/district would select the multiple-intelligences model as one that would be adopted by a school/district. These schools are usually ones that are already failing by the measures used by our society to identify high- and low-performing schools. They are usually ones that score in the lower end of state and national assessments. They are usually the ones with the highest retention rates and the highest dropout rates. They are usually ones that have a high proportion of at-risk high-poverty students. These schools, and the teachers, staff, students, and parents that inhabit and populate them, have been bombarded for 15 years with what have become almost daily media accounts of how our public schools are failing. These are the same professionals who have tried the traditional and the nontraditional approaches with difficult-to-educate children with little success. These are people who, like most educators, feel deeply about their students and who want them to succeed but who have not found the approach that elevates student learning to acceptable levels. The theory of multiple intelligences makes perfect sense to them. The children they teach cannot excel in the traditional modes of schoolwork, i.e., the linguistic and logical/mathematical intelligences. However, they can excel in one of the other intelligences. In my opinion, the theory has been embraced in many instances because it provides a raison d'être for failure in the traditional school areas. The teachers, administrators, staff, parents, and students are not failures because the intelligences of these children lie in areas not assessed by state or national measurements.

To be sure, this is again a gross oversimplification. There are wonderful examples of multiple-intelligence schools that have been very successful and that have dramatically increased student achievement. The Key Renaissance Middle School in Indianapolis is the best-known example. However, the numbers of such schools with documented increases in student achievement is low. Instead, most such schools espouse the very opposite philosophy of increasing student achievement in traditionally measured ways. They do not care about such achievement. Instead, they point to the other intelligences and how their students perform in those areas. Of course, it is extremely hard to measure success in those other areas in comparison to students enrolled in a traditional or non–multiple-intelligences school. Therefore, you have no real way of measuring success. Even the Key School had to alter its approach to get off its district's academic probation list when almost half of its student body scored below average on basic skills as assessed by the Indiana Statewide Testing for Educational Progress (ISTEP).

A second reason most multiple-intelligences schools continue to languish in low achievement is the difficulty of transforming a theory into effective daily lesson plans. The feat of attempting to teach to eight totally different intelligences is

staggering by itself. How this is often done is to have one concept taught by rotating students through eight different stations or centers. Although this is often fun, it is extremely
time-consuming. Precious time on task is taken away from
whole-group instruction, which the effective schools research
indicates is both efficient and effective. Other multiple-intelligences approaches are used more effectively. For example,
students are given an option as to how they want to report to
the class on some research they have done. One student may
report in a paper-and-pencil format. Others may sing their reports. Others may build models to illustrate their findings.
Others may act theirs out. This is an effective use of a multiple-intelligences approach. In reality, this is merely an elaboration of the learning-styles approach, which predates multiple intelligences. It is sound pedagogy to use a variety of
teaching styles and a variety of learning styles in our schools.

A third problem with the multiple-intelligences approach
is the de-emphasis it places on skills that are absolutely vital to
success in life. Everyone in our modern society needs to read,
write, speak, and listen well, and must have an extensive understanding and grasp of mathematics and science concepts.
It is far too easy to label a student as not having ability in these
vital intelligences and to expect too little of them. Virtually all
students can read at grade level, and most all students can
conquer the intricacies of algebra and geometry. Too say that
students' intelligence lies in the physical arena to the exclu-
sion of the more useful and essential intelligences is detrimental to the students' achievement. We should not ignore the tal-
ents and abilities of students in all of the many different
intelligences, but to do so at the diminution of the importance
of those intelligences that lead to the acquisition of competent
language and mathematical skills is harmful and should not
occur.

A personal example of what can happen when a multiple-intelligences approach is used in a school, and what can
happen when it is abandoned, will illustrate the dangers of the
approach and the advantages of others. In a school district
with 16 elementary schools in which I served as superintendent, one school consistently stood out as underperforming. It

had the greatest percentage of students receiving free and reduced-price lunch and scored lower than any other school in
the district on the Iowa Test of Basic Skills (ITBS), which was
the nationally-normed assessment used by the district. It had
a ten-year track record of being the school in the district with
the lowest achieving students. The school switched from a traditional elementary model to a multiple-intelligences model.
It became well known in the state and region for utilizing this
new approach. It had strong supporters from a number of pro-
fessors at the local regional university. It was touted as a
school to be modeled and emulated. It even held its own regional conference in conjunction with the local university. The
conference was successful. They shared the multiple-intelligences approach, the school became even more widely
known, and both the school and the university made a small
amount of money from the conference. One university professor who had worked closely with the school announced at the
conference's luncheon that this was the finest school he had
ever seen. However, achievement levels remained the same;
no improvement was forthcoming.

Because of the lack of the school's success, and because it
and a nearby school were at half capacity, the district decided
to combine the two schools and to create a new, reconstituted
magnet or choice school. As expected, the neighborhoods ob-
jected to the combining of the schools and requested an opportunity to create two choice schools in an effort to attract students from other nearby schools. Permission was granted to
the schools as long they selected or developed models that
best practice and educational research indicated should improve student achievement. One and a half years later, a new
principal, Kathy Malvern, took over the reins of the school.
She immediately started working with staff to jettison the
multiple-intelligences approach and to research together
school restructuring models that made a difference in student
achievement. After six months of study, the school adopted
Henry Levin's Accelerated School Model out of Stanford University. In just one year, and without significant new financial
resources, the school improved its ITBS student scores by 13
percentile points and its school score by 23 percentile points.

The difference between the anticipated achievement score based on the Cognitive Abilities Test (COGAT), which was administered at the same time as the ITBS, and the actual ITBS achievement score was staggering. The difference of a negative -0.4 the previous year shot up to a positive +0.3. For the other grade assessed, the school maintained and even slightly increased its ITBS scores of the previous year. However, the difference between the COGAT and the actual ITBS score for that grade was also impressive. From a negative -0.1 the difference rose to a positive +0.6. To put this in better perspective, Riverside Publishing Company, which owns the ITBS, indicates that a difference of 0.4 is significant. The school is continuing to learn and utilize the Accelerated School Model and to continue its transformation from a school that was failing its students to one that is eminently successful. There were many reasons why the school has turned around. The Accelerated School Model is not the only reason, but it is a significant one. One thing is for sure: it could never have reversed itself if it had retained the multiple-intelligences model.

Middle School Philosophy

Some people argue that the decline in student achievement in American public schools can be traced back to the advent of middle-school education. As the middle-school philosophy became in vogue, and more and more students were shifted out of a junior high school model, the lower student achievement sank. There may be some truth to this assertion, but the decline of student achievement in America has been the result of many factors and certainly should not be laid at the doorstep of middle-school education. The philosophy that the middle years should be a transition between the protected, less stressful and less demanding elementary grades and the homework-laden, rigorous academic and more adult high-school environment seems to be reasonable and logical. The philosophy that students should be exposed to a number of exploratory subjects in the middle grades to better determine the appropriate path for high school also seems to have merit. The belief that middle-school-aged youngsters are transitioning from childhood to adulthood with all of the accompanying social, emotional, and physiological changes is, without question, true. Does all of this mean that middle-school students cannot, or should not, be expected to make significant academic progress? The answer to this is a categorical "no." Unfortunately, as is sometimes the case in other areas of education, we appear to have taken an original, good idea and swung the pendulum too far. In this case, we have swung the pendulum too far away from an emphasis being placed on academic achievement. In many locations, middle schools are not viewed as a place where the mission is academic learning and achievement. Instead, they are places where the mission is to facilitate the transition from childhood to adolescence. Learning in the core academic areas has taken a back seat in many middle schools. Achievement in the nonacademic areas has become of much more importance. This is not as it should be, and, if achievement is to be raised significantly in the middle grades, there must be a return to an academic emphasis during these critical years.

This rigid adherence to the middle-school concept at the expense of student learning was stated very well by Ronald D. Williamson, an assistant professor at the University of North Carolina at Greensboro, and J. Howard Johnston, a professor at the University of South Florida, in *The School Administrator*. They note that hundreds of middle-school faculties have adopted the orthodoxy of the middle-school model and that they cling to the established model without regard to student learning. Such faculties believe that success is measured by whether or not the school has the components of the middle-school model such as "the existence of instructional teams, advisory programs, interdisciplinary units, block schedules, intramural programs..." In their opinion "program characteristics have become primary and student success has assumed a secondary role."

The changes that need to be made in many middle schools are one of degree. Wholesale changes away from the middle-school philosophy are normally not required. However, a thorough analysis of how middle schools operate in a district is in order. Changes can then be made that are customized for individual schools/districts that will maximize student achievement without moving completely away from the middle-school concept/philosophy. Many of the needed changes have already been summarized in other sections of this book. However, because of the importance of these items to the middle-grade years, and because of the unique steps that apply only to this school level, each item is covered again here. This redundancy is meant to assist the reader by organizing all of the unique facets of the achievement elements as they apply to middle school in one place.

♦ Determine Minimum Time on Core Areas

This is of particular importance to middle school because of the myriad of exploratory subjects offered. It is a safe practice to use the same minimum time that a district has determined is needed in the elementary and the high schools, at the middle level as well. Resistance will probably occur because of the entrenched belief that a little bit of every exploratory is more important than time spent on the academic core.

An example of how strongly entrenched the noncore academic areas are in middle school can be seen in the music/band program. It is not unusual for music/band to be treated differently from every other exploratory course. Whereas most all other exploratories last for only a trimester or semester, music/band lasts all year. For a student to take band, he must give up the opportunity to take some other exploratories. Because music is something enjoyed by most students, particularly at this age, many students opt to take music/band for the year. Music/band teachers perpetuate the need for music/band to be taken every day, all year. It strengthens their program and makes students better performers. Nonetheless, a yearlong band/music program is contrary to the middle-school philosophy where it is espoused that students should be introduced to many different exploratories.

The hold that music/band has over even academic subjects is remarkable. In one district where I worked, we introduced foreign language in kindergarten in most of the elementary schools. This, of course, had a profound effect on the district's middle schools because many students were expected to continue their mastery of the language while in middle school. Thus, the exploratory foreign language classes, which were little more than a short ten-week introduction to the culture of the countries that used the language, had to be replaced by true foreign language instruction. Schools recognized the direct conflict that was bound to occur between music/band and foreign language, both of which were structured as yearlong daily classes. Some schools attempted to pit the two against one another by forcing students to choose between music/band and foreign language. This does not need to occur, but it does mean that one must view music/band in a different manner than is customary in most middle schools. In my opinion, foreign language should take precedence over music/band because it is a part of the academic core. If it requires daily, yearlong instruction, students should never be forced to choose between an academic core subject and a noncore subject. This lessens the overall academic achievement. Fortunately, there are solutions to these potential conflicts, but if traditional teachers and administrators choose to draw a battle line between core academic subjects and noncore areas, the academic core must win the battle if the school wishes to increase student achievement.

♦ Realign Purpose of Noncore Areas

Again, this is as important at the middle grades level as it is at the other levels.

♦ Increase Length of Day

One way for exploratories at the middle-years level to be offered and still insist on a full academic load is to extend the length of the school day. An additional one to three exploratories can be added per year by simply extending the length of the day by thirty minutes for students.

♦ Increase Length of Year

In the same way that more exploratories can be offered to students by extending the school day, more exploratory time can be gained by lengthening the school year.

♦ Require Regular, Consistent, Quality Homework

I believe that this is one of the most critical elements at the middle-school level. A significant ratcheting up of outside independent work can be expected of young adolescents to a greater level than is currently the case. It is also a critical time to establish and cement the work ethic of young people. If good work patterns and the acceptance of responsibility can be established in middle school, the likelihood of it continuing into high school and beyond is greatly enhanced. Just as likely is the continuation of poor work habits if they are established at this age.

♦ Increase Graduation Requirements or Eliminate Social Promotion

It is important to establish the link between successful work in middle school and promotion to high school. Indeed, it is important to link successful schoolwork to promotion to higher grades at all school levels, including elementary schools. The problem of social promotion is not a small one. In research reported by the United States Department of Education in the May 1999 publication entitled *Taking Responsibility for Ending Social Promotion*, more than 50 percent of teachers had promoted unprepared students during the previous year. Other research indicates that 10 to 15 percent of all high school graduates are unable to balance a checkbook or write a cogent letter to a company explaining an error on a bill. Yet, only approximately 3 percent of students are two or more years over age for their grade, which is a strong indication that a child has been retained.

It is not a wise practice to retain students. The research is crystal clear as to the negative effects that retention has on students. The dropout rate for retained students is significantly higher than for those who are not retained. Indeed, the correlation between retention rate and dropout rate is very high, leading many to believe that retention may be one of the greatest causes of students eventually dropping out of school. The above report agrees. It notes that although a debate has raged over the years regarding social promotion, we know that neither retention nor social promotion is appropriate. Retaining students without somehow changing the instructional methodologies or strategies does not assist students and does not improve performance.

Nonetheless, it is important for students to understand that they can and will face consequences if they have the innate ability but fail to do the required work. Any middle-school teacher or administrator can relate stories about students who believe that they will move on to high school regardless of the amount of work they do while in middle school. It is viewed as a right that cannot be taken away from them by the school/district. In many cases the students are seemingly correct. They know that they will be passed along to high school regardless of the amount of work or the quality of work they do in middle school. If schools/districts do this, it teaches students that a good work ethic is not necessary to succeed in school and, ultimately, life after school. Therefore, some sort of policy, which establishes consequences for middle-school students who fail to complete the required work, should be in place.

The debate about whether there should be some sort of alternative placement for such students can and should occur in the school/district. A special school, separate from high school and separate from middle school, may be one alternative. Another may be that students move on to the high school setting but are prevented from taking normal high-school coursework until they take and successfully complete the work that was expected at middle school. Another alternative may be retaining the students at the middle school but in an isolated program until they demonstrate mastery of the material they were expected to learn. I am convinced that unless a minimum level of quality work is required at the middle-grades level, the overall achievement of students will be lowered. Students do see and learn from others. They must see the natural negative consequence of failing to complete work of which they are capable, as well as the natural positive consequence of completing such work.

♦ Introduce Weighted Grades

This should not be applicable to middle school. However, there is probably something to be said about the negative impact that occurs when a middle school has a large percentage of its students on honor rolls. Grade inflation has been much written and talked about in this country for a long time. One side of the argument is that you should encourage students by having as many students as possible achieve success. The other side argues that you should use the bell curve to assign grades, thus sorting students into those that can and those that can't. For maximum achievement, a middle ground needs to be reached. Students' work should be held to high expectations, and the expectations should not be artificially lowered. Most students will work to the level expected. However, the achievement of students should not be expected to fall along an artificial bell curve. Indeed, if schools/districts do what is asked of them, virtually all students will learn. Thus, achievement should be skewed to the right. If not, we need to go back and reteach the material until students have mastered it.

Each school/district will need to determine what it considers to be quality work worthy of elevated grades. However, situations where 75-80 percent of the entire student body is listed on an honor roll must be avoided. When that happens, everyone, including the students, knows that such a list is meaningless and is not truly reflective of those students who consistently perform quality academic work. As superintendent, it was my practice to send a personal signed congratulatory letter to all students in middle school or high school who made the schools' honor rolls. In one district, I had to temporarily stop sending these letters to middle-school youngsters because the number of students was too high. It became obvious to me that it was impossible for that percentage of students to be at such a high mastery level.

◆ **Establish Nonschool Tutorial Programs**

Because middle school is the last good chance to capture students who are failing and to make them successful in school, tutorial programs are particularly important. Once in high school, or even once in the upper middle-school grades, the ability to remediate academic problems is nearly impossible.

♦ **Use a Standards-Based Approach**

This is pertinent to middle schools and should be a vital part of increasing achievement at this level.

♦ **Align Vertical Curriculum**

Again, this is as critical in middle school as it is at the other grade levels.

♦ **Introduce Harder Subjects Earlier**

This is especially important for middle schools. In the mathematics area, both algebra and geometry should be provided and all students should be expected to complete one or both by the end of middle school. This is an area where strong resistance may be forthcoming. This is true even in schools/districts that are perceived as high-achieving. Many middle schools believe that students are not ready for the more abstract algebraic and geometric concepts. Thus, the schools keep them engaged in the same mathematics topics that they should have mastered years before. Unless the school/district removes these lower-level courses from the upper grades middle-school curriculum, teachers will continue to put students in those classes instead of the more advanced algebra and geometry courses. A compromise solution may be to install pre-algebra courses as a precursor to algebra for those students who are not as advanced as others. However it is done, harder mathematics material should be expected and required of virtually all students. This is consistent with our foreign competitors' introduction of such material into their national curriculum at earlier grade levels.

Other advanced courses should also be standard fare for middle schools. This is especially true for the sciences and foreign language. I am a strong advocate for the teaching of a foreign language beginning in kindergarten. The advancement of the mastery of the language taught in elementary schools should continue in middle school, or the introduction of a third language should begin. In regards to science, either biology should be taught or the typical science classes offered in middle grades can continue, but the material should become more rigorous.

♦ **Prevent Regression to Easier Subjects**

This is not applicable to middle school.

♦ **Eliminate Approaches That Lead to Lowered Achievement**

These approaches are not typically used in middle schools. However, the harmful effects of these approaches used in elementary schools may very well require some remediation efforts at the middle-school level until these approaches are eradicated in earlier grades.

♦ **Teach What Is Tested and Test What Is Taught**

This is just as true for the middle years as elsewhere in the educational system.

In addition to these modifications in our middle schools a number of other areas need to be examined. These suggested modifications follow.

♦ **Direct Reading Instruction**

In many middle schools, it is typical that reading is no longer taught except to students who are significantly behind. As educators, we assume that students know how to read by the time they get to middle school. Therefore, direct reading instruction is rarely taught except in a remedial fashion. My experience has taught me that virtually all middle-school students still need direct formal reading instruction, especially in reading comprehension. In two districts where I worked, achievement in reading comprehension rose dramatically when all students in the middle schools were given direct reading instruction. In addition, achievement in reading mechanics, word attack skills, fluency, and speed, as well as other areas, also rose significantly.

♦ **Writing**

Another area of the curriculum that is insufficiently taught in the middle grades is writing. Writing is one of those skills that can get progressively better and better, but only if sufficient time is spent writing, and only if proper instruction and feedback are provided. It is almost impossible to spend too much time on writing. We must spend more time in our middle schools on writing instruction, even if that means we spend less time on noncore academic areas.

◆ Home Economics

Finally, there are some traditional subjects that need to be eliminated from our middle school (and high school) curriculum. Chief among these is home economics. Once upon a time, when homemaking was the primary occupation of women in America, it might have made sense to teach home economics in our public schools. This is no longer the case. This does not mean that many of the skills taught and the information conveyed in home economics are not useful. They are. However, is it the place of public schools to teach such information? If there is one area that can be best taught at home, is it not home economics? In my opinion, it is not the responsibility of public school education to teach home economics skills to students when we are still failing to teach all of our students how to read, write, and calculate properly. This does not mean that home economics cannot be modified into meaningful occupational education classes. It can. The food industry is huge, and many people can pursue wonderful occupations in this important industry sector. But the classes students need in these areas are so radically different from teaching students to sew on a button or to boil pasta that they no longer resemble home economics.

◆ Industrial Arts

Another traditional area that needs significant modification is the "shop" class. It is important that we continue to have the traditional building/construction trades taught in our schools, although an apprenticeship model designed after the system used in Germany is far more preferable than the way we teach these skills. The old traditional "shop" class needs to be replaced by classes using modern technology. These are the types of jobs that will be available to students graduating from our schools in the twenty-first century. Many commercial programs are available on the market today. Tech Lab 2000 is an excellent example. I have helped install these labs in three separate school districts. Achievement went up, as did the motivation and interest of the students. Achievement went up because of the close link between these classes and the academic core areas. Students could see that what they were learning in academic classes could be used in real-life occupations and real-life problem solving.

♦ Trained Math and Science Teachers

One very significant reason why mathematics and science achievement has dropped over the last 20 years may very well be the shift to teachers who are primarily trained in middle-school education and only secondarily trained in mathematics or science itself. Of course, this resulted from the country's shift away from a junior-high-school philosophy to a middle-school philosophy. Educational research done by Goldhaber and Brewer, as well as Darling-Hammond, seems to clearly indicate that student achievement in mathematics is increased when students are taught by teachers who have a bachelor's or master's degree in mathematics, and achievement in science increases when students are taught by teachers with bachelor's or master's science degrees. The 1999 *TIMSS Mathematics Benchmarking Report* notes a correlation between the United States' lower performance in mathematics and the percentage of teachers having degrees in math. Specifically, only 41 percent of eight-grade students in the United States have teachers with math degrees whereas 71 percent of all international students have such degreed teachers. Similar comparisons were found in the 1999 *TIMSS Science Benchmarking Report*.

The TIMSS Benchmarking studies also revealed some surprises regarding the confidence American middle-school teachers felt regarding their preparation and ability to teach math and science. A whopping 75 percent of American teachers that participated in the study felt well prepared to teach eight-grade mathematics, and an even larger 87 percent of all American teachers who teach middle school math were confident of their preparation. This compares to only 63 percent of international teachers. On the other hand, only 27 percent of all American middle-school teachers who teach science believe they are very well prepared. Finally, the lower-scoring United States districts that participated in the 1999 TIMSS study had teachers that reported relatively high levels of confidence in their preparation. The report suggests that this may result from the possibility that the lower scoring districts taught a much less demanding science curriculum.

It seems clear that if a school/district wishes to significantly increase middle-school student performance in both mathematics and science, it would be highly advisable to employ only math and science trained teachers to teach those subjects.

In summary, the extent that each middle school needs to make changes will be different for each school, but significant increases in achievement can be realized by closely examining and changing the practices that detract from achievement that are used by the school.

3

Establish Supportive Accountability

Face the Fear of Accountability

Student achievement cannot be increased to any significant degree without accountability. It is an essential element of performance, and any attempt to raise achievement without accountability is a mostly fruitless endeavor.

Not surprisingly, accountability is often resisted by educators, but is generally supported by those in the general public. This was highlighted in 1998 in the second annual *Reality Check*, a public opinion poll and report, conducted by Public Agenda. It surveyed a number of groups regarding the viability of several accountability proposals. What it found was a growing disparity between the opinions of public educators and the public in general. Part of the results of this poll is reflected below.

Percent Saying Accountability Proposals are a "Good Idea"

	Tie financial incentives for teachers and principals to student achievement	Replace principal tenure with contracts that would be terminated if schools failed to reach specific goals	Overhaul persistently failing schools by replacing teachers and principals and keeping them under strict observation
Employers	60%	77%	66%
Parents	53%	70%	62%
Professors	32%	57%	46%
Teachers	22%	33%	28%

Accountability means different things to different people. To most, the term means responsibility. To be accountable for something, one is responsible for it. This is quite accurate. However, the term also carries a connotation that a consequence will follow if one does not adequately take care of the responsibility. This is also accurate. This is the part that most educators, like most people, fear. This is natural. This is just being human. Accountability carries an implied threat. If you fail to do the job adequately, you will be fired. Thus, job security and personal safety are tied up in the term accountability. When job security is at stake, emotions run high, and that is exactly what one can expect when accountability is introduced into a school/district.

Allan Odden defines accountability in a similar manner. He writes that, "Accountability means a) you identify your most valued results, b) you measure them, and c) you provide incentives or sanctions." Accountability efforts often fail because educators "… back off. They say, 'We don't know what [our most valued results] are, we can't measure them, and we're not going to provide incentives or sanctions.' That means there's no accountability, which means you can do anything—or nothing."

The truth is that most people in most industries do not lose their jobs when they are held accountable. This is true for educators as well. As W. Edwards Deming believed, the vast majority of people are competent individuals who want to do a good job and will do so if given a chance and if given the proper training, materials, and resources to accomplish the job. Thus, most people will perform up to an acceptable level if given the opportunity. However, this truth does not remove the fear of accountability. Therefore, this fear must be faced directly and ways found to alleviate it when accountability is introduced. What must not happen is that the fear of accountability and the resistance of those who fear it prevent accountability measures from ever being formulated and implemented.

There are two basic approaches to implementing accountability that can be taken. The first can be likened to a military frontal assault with little or no artillery or air support. The group is told what they must do but are not provided maps of the area, are not given intelligence as to the number and fire power of the enemy, are not given the necessary equipment or manpower, and are not given adequate training for the type of terrain in which they will fight. A court martial awaits those who fail to capture the enemy's position. This is the approach taken by many schools/districts and/or state legislatures. Unless all other measures have been attempted and failed, this approach will not increase student achievement. Only in those cases where the group is competent but refuses to accept its responsibility to increase student achievement should such a military frontal-attack tactic be used.

The second approach is a direct one as well. The purpose of the mission is clearly outlined for the group. However, all of the things that are missing in the first approach are included in the second. People are given the necessary resources to do the job that is expected. This is what I refer to as "supportive accountability." Artillery and air support are given as well as the equipment necessary to launch and sustain an attack. If fewer resources are available, then less must be expected of the group or everyone must be prepared for probable failure. In this analogy, if only limited artillery and air support can be provided, then the success of the mission will be lowered. Similarly, proper intelligence, direction, maps, and training must be provided for the mission to succeed. Again, without them, everyone must brace for limited success or for ultimate failure. To demand success without providing the necessary and required resources is a fool's folly. However, it is the norm when enemies of public education demand performance without providing the necessary resources to accomplish the task to the degree they demand. Without a doubt, student achievement can be increased by significant amounts without additional resources. However, there is an end to how much achievement can be raised without shifting and/or adding more resources. Figurative court martials should not await educators who are competent at what they do and who honestly desire to increase student achievement, but who are not provided the necessary resources to do so. When adequate resources are provided and student achievement does not increase to reasonably expected levels, then court martials are in order. The trick is in gauging the competence and attitudinal level of everyone involved and the amount of resources required to do the job.

I have been asked on a number of occasions if principals and teachers should be held accountable for increasing student achievement. Behind the question was the unspoken fear of job loss. Ultimately, teachers, principals, central-office personnel, and superintendents are responsible for student achievement. Indeed, all parties within the education community, including boards of education, are responsible for student achievement. If adequate time and resources are provided and achievement does not meet reasonably expected levels, then those responsible must seek, either voluntarily or involuntarily, occupations for which they are better suited. For the vast majority of educators, job security is not an issue because they will be successful in addressing student achievement. As educators, we must embrace accountability—not fear it. Only then will the critics of public education—who no longer are willing to provide support because they believe that the accountability that should accompany such support is lacking—be willing to listen to educators.

Become Results-Oriented

The first step toward accountability is to become results-oriented. This is an essential step to increasing student achievement. Without it, one continuously flounders in a sea of unmeasurable anecdotal evidence that does not lend itself to true verification of performance. Anecdotal evidence may make one feel good about oneself, but it is useless as a practical means of knowing whether or not you are achieving the objective at hand.

To reflect the importance of data, I always posted the assessment results of the various schools within my district on the walls of my office. It is a clear demonstration to everyone that what matters are results. I learned this from John Murphy who was the former superintendent of Prince George's County in Maryland and of Charlotte-Mecklenburg School District in North Carolina. When he was in these districts, John took steps that dramatically improved achievement. For example, while John was in Prince George's County, student achievement went from 21st out of 24th in Maryland to 10th. Similar results occurred in Charlotte-Mecklenburg. John's book, which he coauthored with Jeffrey Schiller, entitled *Transforming America's Schools,* offers many insights into the changes that are necessary to improve student achievement. On the matter of results and assessment, these authors note that it is the responsibility of the superintendent (and I would add principal) to convey that it is not an unnecessary burden to collect data in all facets of student learning and that such data will improve the capacity of all staff to do their jobs more effectively. They iterate this by writing that school/district restructuring must be data-driven and that educational leaders must have constant feedback concerning the condition of their school/district if achievement is to increase.

The power of becoming results-oriented is also strongly reflected in a wonderful book entitled *Results: The Key to Continuous School Improvement* written by Mike Schmoker and published by the Association for Supervision and Curriculum

Development. Schmoker notes that educators avoid data out of fear. He puts it in the following way:

> Why do we avoid data? The reason is fear—of data's capacity to reveal strength and weakness, failure and success. Education seems to maintain a tacit bargain among constituents at every level not to gather or use information that will reveal where we need to do better, where we need to make changes. Data almost always point to action—they are the enemy of comfortable routines. By ignoring data, we promote inaction and inefficiency.

This fear of data is directly linked to the fear of accountability. Data are merely the source of documenting whether or not the job is being done adequately. People, who fear accountability, fear data. But, without data, there can be no meaningful improvement. Improvement without data is accidental, and accidental improvement cannot be replicated where it is needed elsewhere. Systemic improvement in a school/district must, therefore, come with examining results and using data to make decisions. This is also noted by Schmoker, who writes, "Evidence shows that schools can and will improve if they gear up to strive for increasingly better results by examining and refining the processes that most directly contribute to designated results."

E. B Fiske, who wrote *Smart Schools, Smart Kids: Why Do Some Schools Work?*, echoes this emphasis on processes that produce results. Fiske noted that the typical school still emphasizes process but not results.

W. Edwards Deming, the father of Total Quality Management (TQM), is perhaps the best-known and publicized proponent of using results to constantly improve the quality of the product or service. Although Deming believed that it was inappropriate to use numerical goals, he was an ardent believer in using data to determine what was being done correctly and what needed to be improved. Deming advocated every imaginable type of statistical analysis. However, S. E. Brigham in an article he wrote for the anthology *Quality Goes to School*, discovered one very important point, i.e., TQM organizations that succeed are those that are concerned with processes only to the extent that they affect results. I advocate the same thing in education. We must use many different measures of many different processes to determine where we need to make changes to maximize student achievement.

I am fond of saying that data are data. They are neither positive nor negative, neither good nor bad. They are simply data. Most people view data as reflective of how well they have done their job. They view data as indications of their worth. If the indication is good, they temporarily feel elated, but they soon start worrying about the next round of data. If it is bad, they feel devalued, and they soon dread the next statistical analysis. What educational leaders must do is to explain the objectivity of data and then convince those in the educational system that the purpose of data is to make improvements in the system. The data must be used to change the reading program, or the length of time spent on reading, or the methodology used to teach reading. In the large majority of cases, data are not reflections of the value of the person or school/district.

Most schools/districts that perform poorly on assessments shun data. They know that data often do not reflect on the quality of instruction occurring in the classrooms. They know that they will be compared to higher-performing schools/districts that have certain natural advantages such as having children from middle/upper-income homes with parents who are supportive of education, who encourage their children to succeed in school, and who provide them with the resources outside of school to help make them successful in school. Instead of accepting assessment results to improve student achievement, many of these schools/districts reject assessment data altogether. This is a serious error that will only lead to continued suppressed achievement. Data must be accepted for what they are. Explanations can and should be given to help translate what the data actually mean, but the data cannot simply be rejected out of hand. To do so, is to forever doom the students of those districts to underachievement.

In summary, it is essential to become results-oriented if student achievement is to be increased. One must use data in a positive constructive manner instead of as a club to browbeat those that are not performing as we would hope. Used appropriately, results are a powerful force for student learning.

Use High-Stakes Assessments

Although the concept of high-stakes assessment is abhorrent to many educators, it is vital to increasing student achievement. Indeed, they are an essential element to elevating achievement. The reason is simple enough. Schools/districts must have a distinguishable goal and there must be a distinguishable way to measure whether or not they are reaching the goal.

Many educators, including myself, believe that assessment should be multifaceted. No one type of assessment, or any one instrument, should be used as the sole determiner of whether or not a student, school, or district is doing well or doing poorly. We should be concerned with a body of evidence that, when taken as a whole, reveals the story behind the data. A triangulation of results from a number of different assessments can verify suspicions about the curriculum and methodologies we use within the school/district. In all of the districts in which I have worked, we have tried hard to have a balanced approach. The chart that follows is an example of the assessment matrix we used in one of those districts.

From this matrix it is easy to see that a variety of types of assessments were used. They included a nationally-normed standardized test, criterion- or standards-based assessments, and performance-based assessments employed at various grade levels. Professional staff mounted strong pressure to remove the nationally-normed test as a part of the matrix. However, such tests have their place within a matrix and should not be eliminated. Some newer assessments, such as the Terra Nova produced by CTB McGraw Hill, can be used as both a nationally normed assessment as well as a criterion-referenced test. Such instruments can be used to validate the results of the more traditional, older assessments on the market today.

Assessment Matrix

Grade	State Standard Referenced	District Norm Referenced	District Criterion Referenced	District Performance Assessment	Building-Level Bodies of Evidence	District/Building Screening and Diagnostic
K–2				K–2: Primary 7-Trait Writing 1–2: Math	Portfolios and Teacher-Selected Assessment	Reading: Menu of Tools
3	Reading	CogAT/ITBS Survey with Computation		Math	Portfolios and Teacher-Selected Assessment	Reading: Menu of Tools
4	Reading and Writing	Terra Nova Reading, Writing, and Math	Terra Nova Reading, Writing, and Math	Math	Portfolios and Teacher-Selected Assessment	Reading: Menu of Tools
5	Math	CogAT/ITBS Survey with Computation		6-Trait Writing and Science	Portfolios and Teacher-Selected Assessment	Reading: Menu of Tools

Grade	State Standard Referenced	District Norm Referenced	District Criterion Referenced	District Performance Assessment	Building-Level Bodies of Evidence	District/Building Screening and Diagnostic
6		Terra Nova Reading, Language Arts, Math, Science, and Social Studies	Terra Nova Reading, Language Arts, Math, Science, and Social Studies	Science and Social Studies	Portfolios and Teacher-Selected Assessment	Reading Diagnostic
7	Reading and Writing	CogAT/ITBS Complete Battery			Portfolios and Teacher-Selected Assessment	Reading Diagnostic Follow-up (Nonproficient)
8	Math and Science	TIMSS: International Norms		6-Trait Writing and Math	Portfolios and Teacher-Selected Assessment	Reading Diagnostic Follow-up (Nonproficient)

Grade	State Standard Referenced	District Norm Referenced	District Criterion Referenced	District Performance Assessment	Building-Level Bodies of Evidence	District/Building Screening and Diagnostic
9		Terra Nova Reading, Language Arts, Math, Science, and Social Studies	Terra Nova Reading, Language Arts, Math, Science, and Social Studies		Portfolios and Teacher-Selected Assessment	Reading Diagnostic
10	Reading, Writing, and Math	ITED Complete Battery		Math	PreACT Option P-SAT Option Portfolios and Teacher-Selected Assessment	Reading Diagnostic Follow-up (Nonproficient)

Grade	State Standard Referenced	District Norm Referenced	District Criterion Referenced	District Performance Assessment	Building-Level Bodies of Evidence	District/Building Screening and Diagnostic
11	Reading, Writing, and Math			6-Trait Writing	PreACT Option P-SAT Option ACT Option SAT Option Portfolios and Teacher-Selected Assessment	Reading Diagnostic Follow-up (Nonproficient)
12	Retest Below Proficient	TIMSS: International Norms			ACT Option SAT Option AP Exams Portfolios and Teacher-Selected Assessment	

Despite the fact that a school/district should strive to achieve balance in its assessment program, and despite the fact that a school/district should use an entire body of evidence to make student and program decisions, it is vital for a school/district to have a designated high-stakes assessment. Usually, the school/district has no choice about this high-stakes instrument. If the state has a statewide measure that is used in all schools/districts and is publicly reported, that instrument becomes the high-stakes test. In some states, it may be a regents examination. In others, it may be a criterion-referenced examination developed by the state itself. In other states, it may be a norm-referenced test that is commercially produced and sold. If a state does not have such an examination, it is important for the district to designate one.

Of critical importance is the fact that the results are well publicized through the print and electronic media. Most educators detest the idea that scores of any test are publicized, usually in a straight-ranking format, thereby comparing one school's scores to that of others. Many people do misuse such information, making incorrect inferences that schools with higher overall test scores are better schools. We know that this is not the case. In many instances, schools that have high test scores are actually adding less value to the educational experience than schools with lower test scores. It is not the test score itself that is so important; rather, it is the progress that the school/district has made and the value the school/district is adding to student learning. Thus, a school that started with low achievement may have done much better than a school with high achievement, even though the low-achieving school may be considerably below the score of the high-achieving school. Nonetheless, unless scores are well publicized, there is no pressure on schools to increase student achievement and, once high, to maintain the achievement. Once again, states that have high-stakes assessments normally release the results in a manner that leads to direct comparison, and the media is only too happy to follow suit by publishing the results. If a state does not publish such information, it is important for the district itself to publish the data it has on its own schools. Otherwise, there is little impetus for change that would lead to increased student achievement.

Initiate Accountability
Via Evaluation

Superintendent

Accountability can be greatly hastened through the use of appropriate evaluation models that use data to establish measurable student achievement goals. This applies to virtually everyone that is involved in the educational organization, but is critical for all of those engaged in the instructional process. It begins with the superintendent of the district, extends to building principals and assistant principals, and winds up at the foot of teachers. Everyone is accountable for student achievement. In well-designed evaluation systems, no one can escape the spotlight of student achievement, but it must start with the superintendent.

Superintendents are the obvious leaders of their school districts. They set the example for everyone else. If the superintendent does not have explicit student-achievement goals, how can it be expected that principals and teachers should have such goals? For increased student achievement to be realized, the superintendent must be the first person held accountable. The validity of this truth has been brought home to me in a very personal way. In districts where I did not have measurable student-achievement goals, my efforts went to those other areas for which I was being held accountable. As a result, student achievement did not rise significantly. In districts where specific, measurable student-achievement goals were a part of my evaluation by the board of education, I concentrated on student learning, and achievement rose correspondingly.

An example or two of personal student-achievement goals that I have had illustrates the level of specificity that is needed. One goal read: "Effective implementation of the reading program by 16 percent reduction of students who cannot read at grade level by third grade as measured by ITBS scores." Another was, "All elementary schools within the district will meet or exceed expectations as measured by the ITBS and COGAT with the average of all elementary schools improving the overall basic and composite scores by one month." As can be seen, these goals were directly related to student achievement, they were clear, attainable, and easily measured. In other years, goals were linked to student achievement through other measures that became available, such as the state's standards-based criterion-referenced examination and were not just tied to nationally-normed assessments. Although I maintained other goals that were not achievement-based, a clear focus always remained on student achievement.

Principals

Once accountability through evaluation has been established for the superintendent, the next critical step is establishing it for building principals. This is absolutely essential in any efforts to increase student achievement. Student achievement cannot be accomplished in any meaningful manner without holding principals directly accountable for the achievement in their buildings. Principals influence everything that goes on in a school. They affect the climate, the cleanliness, and the quality of staff. They affect the taste of the food in the cafeteria, the availability of extracurricular athletics and activities, and the general appearance of the building. They also affect student achievement regardless of the socio-economic background of the students. It may not be too much of an overstatement to say that students succeed or fail because of the principal. If the principal does not view the primary mission of the school to be student achievement, then teachers also will not view it as important, and student achievement will suffer as a result. This is true for schools that score very poorly on assessments and for those that score well because of the background of the students who attend the school. Ergo, principals must be held directly accountable for student achievement in their buildings.

There are many different methods of holding principals accountable. In one of the districts in which I served as superintendent, accountability was accomplished through a formal board accountability policy. Since this district already had established a school improvement accountability process, we decided to attack the principal accountability piece through this process. The language of the policy follows.

Policy

Commitment to School Improvement
for Student Academic Achievement

The Board of Education recognizes that in order for a school to improve student academic achievement, there needs to be a systemic way of knowing how each school is performing and how each school can improve. School improvement accountability is a process to ensure that schools meet expectations for increased student academic achievement. The school improvement accountability system consists of the following elements.

A School Advisory Accountability Committee will be established at each school in compliance with state law and accreditation guidelines and will be representative of the community's diverse ideas.

Based on data from the most recent Accountability report, the School Advisory Accountability committee will make recommendations for school improvement goals.

School improvement goals will be developed by the principal, the Deputy Superintendent for School Management and Accountability, and the Superintendent. The goals will align with the Board of Education's goals and may include recommendations from the School Advisory Accountability Committee. The Superintendent will have final approval of all school improvement goals.

Goals will be established in a specific school improvement goal area with expected progress, objective measures, and rewards for exceeding goals defined.

Central Office administration will assist in the school improvement process in every way possible. Ultimately, the principal is responsible for the school improvement process and goal accomplishment.

At the end of the school year, the principal, the Deputy Superintendent for School Management and Accountability, and the Superintendent will evaluate the achievement of goals.

Each school will be responsible for the annual reporting of school improvement goal accomplishments in a consistent format to the school community.

It is expected that there will be ongoing significant school improvement within a two-year time period.

The Board of Education shall adopt and maintain a school improvement accountability system that meets all of the requirements of the Rules of Accreditation of Schools. The Board of Education further recognizes that the responsibility for a child's social, emotional, physical, and intellectual development lies primarily with the family and the student. To that end, student/parent responsibility is a component of the school improvement accountability system. Accountability for student performance is the responsibility of parents, students, and staff.

Every effort shall be made by the Board of Education, the Superintendent, the principal, the staff, the parents, and the students to fulfill the responsibilities inherent in the school improvement accountability process.

The following are the administrative procedures that accompany the accountability policy.

Administrative Procedure

Commitment to School Improvement
Accountability for Student Academic Achievement

In-service

The Deputy Superintendent shall provide a school improvement accountability orientation to all school administrators prior to the commencement of the school year.

Components of Orientation:

1. Copies of adopted school improvement standards shall be distributed.
2. School improvement standards shall be discussed in depth.
3. The school improvement accountability process and time line will be explained.

School Improvement Performance Standards

The school improvement performance standards are the expectations that the Board of Education and the Superintendent have for the school improvement goals. Goals may be set in four standards. The standards for goal setting and the number of goals in each standard will be determined in the goal-setting process.

The four school improvement performance standards are:

♦ Student Performance
♦ Educational Programming
♦ School Learning Climate
♦ Parent/Student Responsibility

Within each of these school improvement performance standards are criteria for goal setting.

Student Performance

The criteria in this area would include any goal that has an outcome of improved or elevated student academic achievement.

Examples: Improvement of student performance on standardized tests; increased literacy; and increased student progress toward meeting or exceeding benchmarks.

Educational Programming

The criteria in this area would include any goal to improve or create educational options that lead to elevated academic achievement for all students or target populations.

Examples: The alignment of curriculum, standards and assessment; remedial reading programs; creative homework programs; extended school year for some students; elementary foreign language programs; school-to-work programs; summer academic enrichment; International Baccalaureate; summer remedial programs; academic co-curricular programs; individualized efforts which make use of IGO's (Individualized Goals and Objectives) and IEP's (Individualized Education Plans); portfolios; student integrated project options; programming to address learning needs of those scoring below proficient; programs to address school curricular weaknesses; gender and ethnic equity programs; and programs which provide appropriate academic challenges for a target group.

School Learning Climate

The criteria in this area would include any goal that targets improved school/learning climate as climate relates to students' academic achievement.

Examples: Improved attendance; establishment of effective discipline systems; establishment of high expectations; recognition of excellence in teaching;

recognition of world-class performance by students; establishment of a school culture that values achievement/progress; and establishment of a safe, orderly environment.

Parent/Student Responsibility

The criteria in this area would include any goal that targets increased parent or student responsibility for elevated student academic achievement.

Examples: Increased parent volunteerism; establishment of homework accountability; increased student participation in a given program or activity; increased attendance; improved communication between home and school; increased parent attendance at school functions; and involvement of parents in instruction or practice with their children. It should be understood that a parent's responsibility is limited to his or her own child or children and that District staff cannot be held responsible for family responsibilities.

The mainstays of this policy and administrative procedure were the four areas in which principals had to establish goals. Whereas only one (student performance) involved actual measurement of student achievement, the other three (educational programming, school learning climate, and parent/student responsibility) were directly linked to learning and, if written and implemented correctly, improvement in these three areas should lead to increased student achievement being measured in the student performance goal area. This turned out to be the case in this district. Every school significantly improved student achievement, and the policy had a direct bearing on that improvement.

Many educators attempt to avoid the responsibility for improving student achievement in an objective and measurable manner. However, once the fact is established that student achievement will be a large part of what will be contained in their evaluation, and once this is accepted, most people will need training on how to write measurable goals tied to achievement. The reason is simple enough—as educators, we have been used to writing goals which are "input" or activity-driven and not "output' or results-oriented. We have become very good at describing activities that we will do to try and reach a goal, but not describe what the result should look like to know if we actually accomplished what we set out to do. We then credit ourselves with having met our goal because we can claim that we accomplished the activities we said we would undertake. One of the biggest hurdles we had as a school district in becoming results-oriented was to shed ourselves of the old habits that activity-based evaluation processes had ingrained in us.

An example will help. Let us assume that school personnel are unhappy with the number of minorities that drop out of school, and, for those who do graduate, they are unhappy with the number who enter a postsecondary college/university. They have scratched their heads over why the percentages are significantly different from the majority population because the demographics of the school's student population are the same for all ethnic groups. The school decides to put into place a program it had been studying called Advancement Via Individual Determination (AVID). AVID is a program specifically designed to intercede with minority students for the purpose of reducing dropouts and increasing the numbers of students attending college. All too often, the goal of the principal would be to secure the necessary funding and to implement the AVID program. The principal would then consider himself/herself successful if he/she actually did wrangle the finances needed (not an easy task) and implemented the program. He/she may feel very good about the program. The principal has talked to the students involved in the program, and the statements they have made are positive and would lead one to think that the program is working. Other people may come to visit the school to see how the program is run and to see if they wish to replicate it in their school. Somewhere in all of the excitement of new program implementation, and the desire for it to be successful, the principal (and supervisor) have forgotten that the goal was not to implement AVID. The goal was to decrease the dropout rate and to increase the number of students entering a postsecondary institution. The goal, therefore, should not be to implement AVID, but to decrease the minority dropout rate and to increase the rate of minority students going to college. AVID is merely a tool to attempt to reach the goal—it is not the goal itself. (By the way, AVID is a very successful program for many schools throughout the country for accomplishing the goals this fictional school had.)

Another example may be of additional help. Let us assume that the goal is "to improve communication." The common trap is for the principal and supervisor to agree to a series of activities the principal will undertake to bolster communication. These may include doubling the number of newsletters the school sends home during the year; the initiation of a series of monthly "coffees" for parents who wish to come to the school to discuss their ideas or concerns; and increasing the number of faculty meetings. Once again, the end result would often be that the principal and supervisor agree that if these things are completed, communication will have improved. Of course, this is not true. Logic may lead us to believe that communication will improve if these three activities are completed, but we have no objective, measurable way of knowing if communication has actually improved. The activities may be undertaken but they are not the goal. The only way for the principal to know if communication was improved is to ask the people with whom he/she is trying to communicate if it has improved. Therefore, the principal may need to conduct a written survey/questionnaire at the end of the year designed to ask just that question. The survey may also inquire as to the reasons communication was better or worse than the previous year. This would determine if the activities the principal undertook actually caused a change in the effectiveness of communication.

A brief but succinct way of thinking about accountability through evaluation is this: It is the outcome and not the process that is important. It makes no difference what activities one undertakes to reach a measurable goal. It is whether or not one reaches the goal that matters. This should not be misinterpreted to say that the means to achieving a goal are not important. They are very important. What it does say is that noble efforts to reach a goal are unimportant if the goal is never reached.

Other Administrators

Whereas the superintendent and principals are the primary administrators who must be accountable for increasing student achievement, every other administrator in a school/ district must also have the goal of improving performance. This applies to people in human resources, finance, maintenance, food service, transportation, and every other department. It applies to direct line administrators, as well as staff positions. It applies to deputy superintendents, assistant/associate superintendents, directors, coordinators, supervisors, managers, assistant principals, athletic administrators, executive assistants, deans, and all other administrators.

Some departments within a school district will have a difficult time in linking their actions to student achievement. Not all will be able to do so in all cases, but most will be able to determine how their actions will improve student learning. It is not difficult to find research that has determined that student achievement is increased when students have had a healthy breakfast and a nutritious lunch. It is not difficult to link attendance to achievement, and, from this linkage, bus drivers have a valid part in making students successful academically. Human resource personnel are critical to the recruitment and employment of well-trained, quality applicants from whom schools may choose teachers, paraprofessionals, and other employees. The finance department is key to efficient expenditure of funds that frees up monies for instruction-related programs.

Although it is important for administrators who are not directly associated with the instructional process to find linkages to student achievement, it is just as important that these same administrators avoid goals that are counter to student achievement. It is common for people to want to excel in their work, and, therefore, to establish goals that elevate the importance of their respective area. For example, it is important for a building to be well maintained and clean. This provides an environment that is conducive to learning and, thus, helps student achievement. However, it would be counter to student achievement if an administrator in the maintenance area determined that the replacement schedule for carpeting was inadequate and needed to be shortened to keep the carpet looking newer, even though the current schedule accommodated the adequate replacement of carpet. Administrators must always keep a wary eye out for the establishment of goals that take resources away from the critical area of instruction.

Teachers

Just as the superintendent and administrators need to be accountable for improved student achievement, teachers must also become responsible for increased student learning. Indeed, building administrators cannot expect students to improve unless the teachers accept such improvement as their responsibility. The fastest and surest way of having teachers accept student achievement as their responsibility is to include it as a part of their evaluation.

Once a school district has established a link between student achievement and principal evaluation, it is a much easier task to establish the same link for teachers. When I worked in a district in Colorado, we were able to have a number of principals and schools begin to include objective student data goals in the evaluation process. Principals had already seen the power such goals could engender in creating a focus for school improvement. However, the task of tying student performance to teacher evaluation was much simplified when a new state law made this mandatory for all schools/districts. Utilizing the law as our guiding requirement, we created a committee composed of teachers to work with the department of human resources to revamp the district's evaluation policy to conform to the state law, while also ensuring that the language and purpose of the policy supported teachers in as positive a fashion as possible. The policy was altered by replacing the vague language, "The district shall maintain an evaluation procedure for all certified personnel with the primary intent of *preserving and improving the quality of learning conditions for stu-*

dents" to the more specific wording, "The district shall maintain an evaluation procedure for all certified personnel with the primary intent of *increasing student achievement and performance.*" This wording had the net affect of significantly altering the evaluation process used with teachers. In the old policy, virtually any action or activity could be claimed to meet the intent of the policy, and, thus, teachers were not wedded to increasing student achievement. However, the new policy made it abundantly clear that the purpose of evaluation was to determine if, and how well, teachers actually increased achievement. In other words, the policy went from the old education paradigm of holding teachers responsible for their activities to a new paradigm of examining results. It went from the input side to the output side. This is a terribly important distinction that will assist any school or district in raising student achievement.

Further wording was added to the policy to provide clarity and to enable the professionals involved to mold the policy to their individual situations. This wording read, "The measurement of the level of performance for certified staff shall include, but not be limited to, a standard for *measuring performance as it is directly related to classroom instruction* and shall include multiple measures of student performance." Because the district embraced the idea that student achievement should be based on a body of evidence and not rely on a single data source or assessment, it was consistent for multiple measurements to be used to determine student achievement and performance. It also made sense not to limit the entire evaluation of teachers' performances to student achievement. Although the policy clearly addressed the primary purpose of evaluation as being student achievement, it did not preclude other purposes. The further wording makes it clearer that the administrator and teacher involved may include other teacher performance measures.

Even with the additional wording in the policy, more specificity was needed to guide the evaluation process. This was done through the administrative procedure that accompanied the policy. The procedure was changed from the following brief wording:

Demonstrates increased student growth and productivity

a. Uses a variety of assessment tools

b. Records students' progress

to the following more descriptive language:

Demonstrates increased student achievement and performance

a. Collects and analyzes student data to drive instruction.

   (1) Collects a variety of student data prior to instruction

   (2) Analyzes and uses data based on individual student and group performance

   (3) Customizes instruction based on analysis of individual student and group needs

b. Uses multiple measures of student performance over time to document student growth

   (1) Uses a variety of selected response (true/false, multiple choice, matching), constructed response (fill in the blank, essay, short answer), performance tasks, or personal communication strategies (discussion, interviews, teamwork, group dynamics, listening.)

   (2) Selects the assessments based on how efficiently and effectively the technique measures the standard proficiencies

   (3) Develops a body of evidence about a student's growth that provides valid, reliable and credible information from which generalizations about student growth can be made

c. Implements strategies based on various types of student achievement data to improve student performance

   Utilizes a comprehensive assessment plan that includes formal and informal data collection (class-

room and school assessments, e.g., anecdotal records, writing samples, student self-evaluations,
checklists, reading assessments; state and district
norm-referenced and standards-referenced assessments.)

d. Analyzes the results of instruction and modifies
instruction accordingly.

Instruction is modified for all students based on a
thorough on-going analysis of data.

As can be seen from the administrative procedure, there
are many ways to determine if teachers are being successful in
increasing student achievement and performance. The old adage that people will pay attention to what is measured is certainly true. By insisting that teachers will be evaluated on student achievement, teachers will concentrate on student
achievement, and student achievement will increase as a result.

Support Personnel

Just as it is important for all administrators and teachers to
be held accountable for student performance, all support personnel in a school/district should also have student achievement as their primary goal. Many support personnel have a
direct link to students. Such staff should have the same goals,
based on the same objective measures, that are used by the faculty with which they work.

Other support personnel that perform functions that are
more removed from direct instruction still play a vital role in
student achievement. Just as it is important for administrators
who are in support positions not to stress the importance of
their areas of responsibility to such a degree that they take
scarce resources away from direct instruction, support personnel must also refrain from this siren call. A prime example
of this came in a district in which I worked. The district emphasized the safety of children getting to and from school.
That is as it should be. However, over time, this emphasis had
created an overabundance of school crossing guards at most
elementary-school sites. The city government actually reim-

bursed the district for crossing guards that city traffic/safety engineers determined were necessary. If the district decided more guards were necessary, it was the district's responsibility to pay for them. Additional crossing guards had been put at virtually all elementary schools for a number of different reasons. For example, heavy construction that blocked sidewalks or that produced heavy traffic volumes may have precipitated additional guards being warranted. However, over time, the original causes for increased guards disappeared, but, of course, the crossing guards did not. When steps were taken to lower the number of guards employed to more closely match the number that the city experts recommended, stiff resistance was met from many different employee groups. The fact that such a large number of crossing guards was not needed and was taking away from resources that could have gone directly to instruction was never a serious factor for those who resisted thinning the ranks of these personnel. This is the very type of situation that must be avoided by support personnel. Their job is to support student achievement and not to detract from it by overemphasizing the importance of their job role.

Develop Financial Incentives

Accountability is the "stick" for increasing student achievement, or, at least, that is the view of many people. Although I have shown that an emphasis on results and accountability does not, and should not, be a negative force for the vast majority of the work force, there is certainly an element of truth to the fact that accountability engenders heightened anxiety. However, this is useful. For years, research has shown that performance increases when anxiety level is heightened but not to such a degree that it becomes debilitating. Just as significant, it is important that anxiety level is neither too low nor elevated over an extended period of time. We all maximize our performance if our anxiety level is at an elevated, but controllable, level.

Just as important to performance are incentives, or the "carrot," that reinforce individuals for increasing student achievement. For most people, the very fact that they accomplish elevated goals that they have established for themselves is rewarding. For all of us, a pat on the back, a kind word, a short note, or public recognition are strong rewards. Without these types of rewards, any job would be mundane at best, and unpleasant or unacceptable at worst. Despite these simple truths, we live in a society that uses money as the primary incentive for most all endeavors. The success of people is often judged by the amount of money they make. Thus, financial incentives are a powerful, driving force for most Americans. If we are financially rewarded for certain results, we tend to want to work toward those results and to avoid activities that lead to results that are not financially rewarded. Educators are not immune from the same psychological forces that drive all other human beings. However, unlike many other Americans, the financial reward system for educators has not been closely linked to productivity. Thus, it is important to provide some sort of financial incentive for improved student achievement. This is supported by Allan Odden's research that indicates that when teachers are given a bonus of $1,000 to $2,000 for increased student achievement, higher test scores are the result. He concludes that bonuses "get the attention of teachers and they improve student achievement in core academic subjects."

Much has been written about financial incentives, merit pay, or performance-pay programs. There are many different ways to provide such incentives. They can be given to individuals or to groups. A small amount of money can be given to large numbers of people, or large amounts of money can be given to fewer people. Incentives can be based on objective measures or on subjective judgment. They can comprise the majority of the pay an individual receives, or they can be a supplement to a larger base salary.

In one district in which I worked, we developed a career-ladder program that was recognized by the American Association of School Personnel Administrators as the best in the country. In two other districts we developed performance-pay programs for building administrators. From these personal experiences, and the research that went into the development of the programs, it appears that there are some best practices that will increase the likelihood of the program being success-ful in raising student achievement.

First, the program should be voluntary. Those few indi-viduals who find the very concept of performance pay offen-sive should have the opportunity of not participating in the program without prejudice. I have found in all cases that the majority of individuals do willingly accept such programs, whereas a small minority does not. Second, the exact amount of the performance pay that each person can receive should be known from the start. A pot of money that will be distributed at the end of the process leads to many problems. Third, objec-tive goals with objective measurements with exact dollar amounts tied to the goals should be used to ensure that every-one knows when individuals have earned performance pay and how much they have earned. Fourth, the individuals and their supervisors should mutually determine the goals that need to be achieved to earn performance pay. Although the supervisor must maintain a high expectation, it is crucial that the employee have the ability to negotiate goals that he/she feels are fair and can be achieved. In education, this last guide-line is particularly important because the students in a given school or classroom might be significantly different from those in other schools or classrooms. Consequently, the de-gree of achievement is not as important as the degree of im-provement. Thus, a school or class may progress more rapidly or to a greater degree than another, despite the latter having more elevated achievement data than the former.

If funds are not available for performance pay for all school/district employees, it is my belief that a performance-pay program should be in place for building administrators, even if the amounts are small. Many people disagree with the concept that some individuals should be eligible for perfor-mance pay whereas others are not. However, it is common-place in private enterprise for those people who are responsi-ble for the overall success or failure of the company to be ac-countable for failure and to reap the benefits of success. Why should schools/districts be any different? Effective-schools research determined many years ago that the principal is the key to the success or failure of a school. Although there are exceptions to this rule, a school rarely succeeds with a poor principal. Likewise, a school rarely fails with a quality principal. Therefore, it is not unreasonable to compensate these individuals more than the teachers who work in the school. The salary structure in virtually all schools/districts is based on this fact. Ergo, performance pay for principals is reasonable even without such pay for teachers or staff in the school.

Why is it important to develop a performance-pay program tied to student achievement for principals? The reason is simple. It focuses the attention of the principal on the primary mission of the school. It reinforces the idea that it is student achievement that is important. This, in turn, leads to increased student achievement and performance.

4

Introduce Cooperative Competition

Start Public Schools of Choice

Of all of the ideas advocated in this book, none will be as controversial as the introduction of competition into the public education system. Perhaps Kenneth Godwin and Frank Kemerer have discovered the reason competition is so controversial. In a recent article in *Education Week* entitled "School Choice Trade-Offs," they wrote, "More than any other educational reform, school choice forces educational policymakers to confront core values and clarify the trade-offs they make." Because it is never easy to question our core values, it is no wonder that competition and choice are so controversial. However, if public education is ever to accomplish the level of student achievement that is needed in this country, competition is absolutely vital. Without it, a district will never raise student achievement to the levels that are possible.

Private schools have been a source of competition for public schools for a long while. However, most individuals are not financially able to afford the tuition costs that go along with private schools. This effectively eliminates private schools as legitimate competition with public schools except for the wealthiest of our citizens.

Vouchers or tax credits are the current poster children of many of the political reformers of education as being the best way to introduce competition. Instead of rehashing the arguments for or against vouchers, I simply argue that vouchers are not necessary if public school districts introduce competition through the establishment of various schools of choice. By a school of choice I mean any school that offers an alternative way of educating children that differs from the traditional neighborhood model that exists in the overwhelming majority of public schools. It could be a charter school in states where charters are legal. It could be a private, for-profit school operated by any number of private companies. It could be a magnet school with a particular focus or program-delivery methodology. It could be a school that serves a neighborhood but delivers education in a nontraditional manner, such as through one of the whole-school reform models currently available. It could be a school within a school or a whole-school model. It could be for elementary, middle, or high school, or a school with grade configurations different from the normal K–5, 6–8, and 9–12. It could be an alternative high school for at-risk students.

This is exactly the approach that we used in one school district in which I served as the superintendent. The approach was extremely successful and controversial at the same time. The district expanded from two to thirteen choices within a two-year period, with a number of additional choices scheduled to come on line. Virtually all of the choices were full with waiting lists after the first or second year. Staff who were committed to the idea or model and were determined to make the school a success, created most of the choices. The result was dramatically increased student achievement for the individual students, for the schools, and for the district as a whole. The need for vouchers simply disappeared in this school district. Parents and students were being provided significantly different choices from which to choose. Former advocates of vouchers became public-school advocates because the choice that they desired was being provided to them. This can happen in any district, although small districts must join forces and provide cross-district choices because of the limitations that small size creates.

The vitally important point is that true choice can be provided in the public sector. There is no need for vouchers or tuition tax credits for true competition to occur. This sentiment is echoed by Evans Clinchy in an article he published in *New Schools, New Communities*. He writes, "We can see the possibility of public school choice, although opposition is still vigorous both from those who oppose all choice and from those who favor vouchers that can be used at private schools, being one of the basic facts of all our public systems. If this were achieved, *all* American parents and *all* of our teachers and principals could choose, from a diversity of public schools, the one believed to be best suited to their educational or professional needs." However, in my opinion, unless public school districts begin to provide choice, they will be forced to do so through the provision of vouchers mandated by state legislatures. Unfortunately, the impetus of the voucher movement seems to be far greater than the impetus for public school districts to provide choice. Either way, at some point in the future, public schools will be forced to compete, and increased student achievement will come with competition.

Many people voice concern about what they view as the pitfalls of competition and view cooperation as a better means to achieving the goals of public education. They contend that more is accomplished through teamwork and cooperation than through competition. Without question, there are many virtues of teamwork and cooperation that should be utilized in schools/districts. The trick is to create healthy competition that uses the advantages that cooperation can bring. I use the term cooperative competition to describe this apparent conundrum. In the school district in which we quickly increased the number of choice schools, principals openly cooperated with one another. They shared ideas they were trying, discussed school models they had read about or observed, and they encouraged one another to "think out of the box." Indeed, thinking out of the box was a huge theme for the school district for the first two years that schools of choice were being created. Many of the points in Mike Vance and Diane Deacon's book, *Think Out of the Box*, were used by management in the district to create new paradigms. The creative thinking was freely shared among colleagues. This synergy and sharing were fostered by the encouragement for schools to create K–12 strands of a common nature and to submit those choice strands of three schools as one complete package to the board of education for approval. Thus, schools were discussing vertical linkage of a common theme, which certainly led to teamwork and cooperation. From my experience, competition and cooperation are not mutually exclusive. They become so only if a zero-sum game is played. If the staff of a school is fearful of losing students to another school through choice, they need to remember that they have the ability to create a choice that will draw students from other schools in equal numbers. It is true that at various times there may be an unequal balance, but, given the incentive to do so, any school can create a program so compelling that it can fill itself with students and have a waiting list of eager young minds who want to enroll in the school but cannot because of space limitations.

It is true that some schools have inherent advantages over other schools in their ability to attract students. A school that has a dense population base close to the school has a built-in advantage. A new school with modern facilities and equipment has an advantage over an older school. A school that has an established positive reputation has an advantage over a school with a neutral or negative one. However, time after time what I have experienced is that it is the nature of the program that compels parents and students to choose a particular school. For example, because they seldom have access to public building bond funds, charter schools are often housed in poor facilities that do not compare to those of their public school neighbors. That does not stop them from being filled to capacity with waiting lists. One charter school in one of the districts in which I was superintendent was housed in portable classrooms. The school had no playground, had a gravel road for a driveway, was on leased property under heavy electrical wires, and was situated in an open field fully exposed to the elements. It had 500 students enrolled, with over 1,000 on a waiting list. It was the program that was compelling—not the related accouterments.

When people choose to go to a particular school, whether it is their normal neighborhood school or a choice school out of their usual attendance zone, there is a deeper commitment to that school and its program. It is natural, therefore, for the students and parents to work harder for academic success than would be the case if they were forced to attend one school and one school only. This is one of the reasons (and an important one) that we experienced a dramatic increase in student achievement when choice was introduced. This cannot be overemphasized. Think about it. As a principal of a school or as a teacher in that school, would you prefer to have children who want to be there or children who have to be there. It is a very powerful force when every single child and every parent chooses your school.

Another huge advantage that choice schools share with private schools is the ability to create and maintain the academic program free of political tampering. When parents investigate a private school to determine if they wish their children to attend, they look at what the school does and does not provide, and make their decision based on what exists. They know what they are going to get before the children attend one day of school. They do not negotiate with the school. They do not indicate that they would like to see the reading curriculum be different from what it is. They do not get to vote on how long the school day lasts. They do not get to determine the foreign language being taught at the school or if one should be taught at all. They do not get to decide if the students wear a uniform or not. In essence, they choose to send their children to the school based on decisions already made by the school. Indeed, part of the power of choice is that students and parents choose the school that best meets their needs. They like the way the school is designed. They like the curriculum being used. They like the athletic and extracurricular activities that are offered. They like the transportation system, or lack thereof, that the school has chosen. However, because all individuals are different, there will usually be things that a parent would change if they could. With a choice school, the parents may wish that something was a little different about the school, but they have no legitimate right to complain and advocate for a change because they chose the school the way that it was designed. This, of course, does not mean that the principal and staff of a choice school should not seek out opinions from their customers; nonetheless, they are empowered to maintain the existing design as long as the school remains full of students. This is extremely empowering to the school. If parents are dissatisfied with the school after a period of time, they can be reminded that they chose to enter the school and they can always choose to leave the school, but the school design will not change to suit their particular desire. Disgruntled parents will leave, and new parents who believe in the design will replace them, thus keeping a constant set of highly satisfied customers.

When we first discussed the idea of creating choice schools within a public school district, we were not sure what the response would be. To advertise the choices, we developed an information roll-out program that included what we referred to as *choice information nights*. The choices that would be available in the following year were described, and parents could choose to go to a series of breakout sessions to learn more about the choices in which they were interested. The first such session was held on what turned out to be a horrible snowy, foggy, winter evening. We were astounded to see an overflow crowd fill a school gymnasium. This was repeated a second and a third time in subsequent evenings. We had to extend the number of such meetings and the preestablished cutoff date because the demand was so great. We were astounded again the following year when this scenario was repeated in meetings to describe the previous year's choices and the new choices for the coming year.

In speaking to these gymnasiums full of parents who wanted to learn about the choices that the district was offering I would always make three points. The first is that choice is innately human and particularly American. As citizens of this country, we have choices in just about everything we do. We choose what clothes we will put on in the morning. We choose which movie we will go see. We choose where we will eat lunch. We choose the type and color of car we will drive. We choose whom we will marry. We choose our church. We choose what we will watch on television. We choose almost everything except the school our children will go to. In America, we have told people where they will go to school. This simply does not feel right to many Americans. The second point I always shared is that people are happier with their school if they can choose it from a variety of options. Research does show a greater level of satisfaction for students, parents, and staff who have selected their school. The third point I made was that achievement and learning will rise if people are allowed to choose their school *and* if the school options are all designed to increase student performance. For example, if all choice schools provide foreign language instruction and their normal neighborhood school does not, then students/parents will choose a choice school if they wish to have foreign language instruction. This increases academic learning and achievement for those people selecting a choice school. If enough students select schools that are out of their neighborhood because of a lack of foreign language, the neighborhood schools will be forced to offer a foreign language. Thus, learning increases for all students. The same process applies to choices that provide uninterrupted blocks of language arts, advanced mathematics coursework, or a rigorous international baccalaureate curriculum. The net result is a more rigorous curriculum that people have freely and voluntarily chosen.

Competition through choice creates tension within a school district. As long as the tension can be controlled, it can be a healthy stimulus to more change and more acceptance of change. If it becomes uncontrolled, the results can be great resistance from those who oppose choice. Regardless of whether the tension is controlled or not, competition will be viewed by many as an attack on public schools. Thus, many people will do whatever is necessary to prevent choice and to keep, or to return to, the status quo. This is particularly true when the staff and parents of neighborhood schools begin to feel the effects of competition. If student numbers begin to decline (and they will for certain schools at certain times) and staff positions that were once full-time become part-time and staff are forced to leave the school or perform functions in which they have no real interest, the heat on choice will intensify. When schools are told by parents that they are transferring to a choice school because of a feature the school has that the current school does not have, the opposition will increase. This is when it is critical for the district to find a method of providing resources and support to help the school that is losing students to redefine itself. This is when cooperative competition comes most into play. The district should be there to help the failing school to reshape itself into a school that people want to attend. It should not, however, help the school to simply maintain itself in the same form that parents have shown they do not want. The important thing to remember is that stiff resistance to competition will occur. Nonetheless, competition must be introduced if a school district is to significantly elevate student achievement.

Magnetize or Focus Traditional Schools

One way of providing competition in school districts is one that has existed for a number of years in a variety of locations. Traditional schools can be magnetized or focused by offering a unique program that attracts students. The magnet- or focus-school concept dates back to the 1960s but really got a significant boost beginning in the early 1970s with the passage of the Emergency School Aid Act (ESAA), which in 1975 became the Magnet School Assistance Program (MSAP). This resulted in the utilization of magnet schools as a court-accepted method of desegregating schools when Buffalo's (New York) plan was approved in 1976. Virtually all subsequent desegregation plans after Buffalo included magnet schools. There are, of course, many examples of magnet schools. Indeed, there is virtually no limit to the types of magnets that can exist. They are limited only to the imagination of those who are allowed to think out of the box. There are schools for the performing arts, technology, math and engineering, the sciences, the health professions, the humanities, the building trades and other traditional vocation education professions, law, and a plethora of other areas. Many of these work very well and do attract students who are interested in the focus area, or who have a particular skill they wish to utilize and strengthen. This was confirmed by a study conducted by Lauri Steel and Roger Levine of American Institutes for Research for the United States Department of Education in 1994. They estimated that at that time more than 60 percent of magnet schools could not accommodate all students who wanted to attend and that approximately 50 percent of all magnets maintain a waiting list.

There is a very important distinction that needs to be made between the traditional magnet programs that have been implemented over the last 30 years and the types of choice magnets or focus schools that I propose and helped put into place in school districts in which I worked. Namely, magnet or focus programs must be designed for increased student achievement. Student performance must be their primary mission. A school cannot be held captive to the specialized interest on which the magnet focuses. This is absolutely critical. Instead, the mission must be to increase student achievement through the use of the interest or area the magnet uses. It is certainly legitimate for the magnet to specialize in its focus area to a degree that traditional schools do not, but that should not be the primary thrust.

An example or two will illustrate the point. A couple of dynamic elementary teachers, Jon Wuerth and Carol Stansfield, approached me in a district in which I was superintendent with the idea of creating a school for fourth graders that would be devoted to the environmental sciences. The school would be located in a pristine section of land that the district owned within a much larger state-owned forest to which we had access. From this germ of an idea by two out-of-the-box thinkers came The School In The Woods choice program, which opened two years later with a waiting list of students to get into the school. It is important to note that the emphasis was to use the sciences as a tool to study and learn all of the district standards and curriculum that all other schools within the district used. They would simply use different methodology, techniques, and motivation to accomplish what others used more traditional methods to accomplish. For example, reading and writing would still be emphasized, but *Walden Pond* might be a piece of literature used to tie reading and writing to science. The mission of The School in the Woods was to increase academic achievement. Learning more about science at the expense of improving reading or math skills was not acceptable. Instead, all of the subjects would be integrated through the sciences to enhance student performance.

Another example was a K–8 Arts and Ideas School that was being created by another visionary principal, Lew Davis. Lew had written a thesis 20 years earlier about creating such a school but had never had the opportunity to make his dream a reality until we started installing schools of choice in the district. The Arts and Ideas School is not the typical movie portrayal of a performing arts school where students practice dance until their lungs burst. Instead, it is a school that uses the arts as the engine for learning the same standards and curriculum that all other schools and all other students must master. Just as The School in The Woods integrates science into all other subjects, the Art and Ideas School integrates the visual and performing arts with all other subject areas to enhance the learning. As Lew is prone to explain, most people remember learning the alphabet through song and not through static rote memorization. It is true that students and parents who are attracted to the arts and who may already be accomplished performers will be drawn to such a school. But it is also true that most students can learn through the techniques used by the school.

As previously mentioned, magnet programs came into being in this country because of the need to find a vehicle to foster voluntary racial integration. There certainly is nothing wrong with this concept. If magnets can assist in integrating our schools, they can certainly be used to achieve that end. However, choice schools, in general, including magnets, should have as their primary mission increased student achievement. This may mean creating multiple magnets of the same or similar type in various locations within the district to make it easier for students to attend. The object is to get as many students as possible engaged in schools designed to maximize student achievement. Hopefully, integration can be achieved at the same time.

Criticism has been leveled at magnet schools because of the expense involved in creating certain types of magnets. Usually, the additional expense is in specialized facilities. This is a fair criticism, and such expense should be avoided in as many instances as possible. However, in most cases such additional expense is really not necessary. If specialized facilities are necessary, then it may also be necessary to forfeit other features that are commonly found in traditional schools. For example, when Lew Davis and his teaching cadre were originally designing the Arts and Ideas School, they gave up a traditional gymnasium for a black-box theater that could serve both purposes. In those instances where the nature of the magnet does cost more than would a traditional school, it is important for the magnet to function as a pilot by being the first to utilize certain cutting-edge equipment, materials, features, programs, or procedures. Thus, they become a test bed for the district as a whole. An example is a technology magnet. All schools within a district will utilize technology to some degree with students. However, a technology magnet may be the first to purchase and use a special software program to see if it does what it claims to do. If not, then the district has saved money by not purchasing the software program for other schools.

Magnet and focus schools can enhance a district's choices to students, parents, and teachers. Choice can energize a traditional school and breathe new life and focus into staff, students, and parents alike. Choice schools can increase student achievement if they are designed to do so and if student performance is the primary mission of the design.

Switch to Whole-School Reform Models

In comparison to previous decades, an explosion of reform models has developed over the last 10 years. These models are often associated with a particular academician and/or university. Thus, they have been bred from our research institutions and stand a better chance of being grounded in a solid theoretical framework as well as empirical data. This, of course, is not always the case. A common thread behind the thinking of most of these models is that they are total or whole-school based. Supposedly, the model cannot be implemented successfully unless the entire school uses it. In addition, the model encompasses all of the aspects of schooling and not just bits and pieces that cannot, in and of themselves, effectively increase achievement. This appears to be sound reasoning. Common beliefs, common understandings, common language, common methodologies, common curriculum, common materials, common assessments, common support, and common training should all lead to uncommon results because such uniformity in a given school has been rare in the past.

In my opinion, one of the most damaging facets of American education is the lack of a consistent national curriculum or methodology. Instead, each state and district and school and classroom is different. It has often been true that when teachers shut the door to their classrooms, they have been able to do whatever they think is best. This approach works well for one year, but learning suffers when students must move to another teacher with a different set of beliefs, training, and methodologies. Gaps in the students' learning naturally occur when there is no consistency from teacher to teacher. This is exacerbated when students move from school to school, district to district, and state to state. Thus, one big advantage that whole-school reform models bring is a commonality to the educational delivery within that school.

The trend to whole-school models does not mean that school-within-a-school models should be ignored. Depending on the situation, a school-within-a-school model may be the only viable option to initiate a reform model or a choice program. For example, most high schools would find it difficult to switch their entire curriculum for all of their students to the International Baccalaureate (I.B.) Diploma model. Yet, the I.B. Program is an exciting rigorous curriculum that should be available in every school district in the country. Such models can work smoothly within a traditional school setting, and schools/districts should not hesitate to use them when it is not possible or desirable for an entire school to participate directly in the model.

What are some of the whole-school reform models that are available to public schools/districts? A coalition of the major K–12 education groups (the American Association of School Administrators, the National Association of Elementary Principals, the National Association of Secondary School Principals, the National Education Association, and the American Federation of Teachers) identified and rated 24 such models that are in use in approximately 8,300 schools nationwide in a joint report entitled *An Educators' Guide to Schoolwide Reform* released in early 1999. Some of these models are quite well known and have existed for a number of years, such as Yale University professor, James Comer's School Development Program, which was founded in 1968. Other models are relative newcomers, such as America's Choice, and have no proven track record. The chart that begins on the next page indicates the rating given to the 24 models.

It should be noted that the authors of some of the models, such as Henry Levin, a Stanford University professor and creator of the Accelerated Schools model, take exception to the report and ratings. His contention is that the report was too heavily biased toward models that had comparison groups and too unbiased toward models that have a long record of increased student achievement. My personal experience tells me that there probably is some truth to that allegation.

Whole-school reform models can be excellent additions to choices that are provided by a school district. There is a certain degree of comfort that comes from being part of a network of schools that have the same beliefs and are using the same methodologies. It also provides an element of credibility to parents who may be skeptical of a school that operates differently from the schools they attended. Like most choice schools, whole-school reform models also provide truly different ways of teaching and learning that may greatly help those children who are not being successful in other models. That was the case we experienced in one of my districts where we were able to install a number of the 24 whole-school reform models.

Ratings of Whole-School Reform Models

Name of program	Evidence of positive effects on student achievement	Year introduced in schools	Number of schools	Support that developer provides to schools	First-year costs	First-year costs with current staff reassigned
Accelerated Schools (K–8)	Strong	1986	1000	Promising	$27	$14
America's Choice (K–12)	?	1998	300	Strong	$190	$90
ATLAS Communities (PreK–12)	?	1992	63	Promising	$98	$90
Audrey Cohen College (K–12)	?	1970	16	Promising	$161	$86
Basic Schools Network (K–12)	?	1992	150	Promising	$12	NC
Coalition of Essential Schools (K–12)	Mixed, Weak	1984	1000	Marginal	NA	NA
Community for Learning (K–12)	Promising	1990	92	Strong	$157	$82

Co-NECT (K–12)	?	1992	75	Strong	$588	NC
Core Knowledge (K–8)	Promising	1990	750	Promising	$56	NC
Different Ways of Knowing (K–7)	Promising	1989	412	Strong	$84	NC
Direct Instruction (K–6)	Strong	1960s	150	Promising	$244	$194
Expeditionary Learning Outward Bound (K–12)	Promising	1992	65	Strong	$81	NC
The Foxfire Fund (K–12)	?	1966	NA	Marginal	$65	NC
High Schools That Work (9–12)	Strong	1987	860	Strong	$48	NC
High Scope (K–3)	Marginal	1967	27	Strong	$130	NC
League of Professional Schools (K–12)	Marginal	1989	158	Promising	$13	NC
Modern Red Schoolhouse (K–12)	?	1993	50	Strong	$215	NC

Name of program	Evidence of positive effects on student achievement	Year introduced in schools	Number of schools	Support that developer provides to schools	First-year costs	First-year costs with current staff reassigned
Onward to Excellence (K–12)	Marginal	1981	1000	Strong	$72	$60
Paideia (K–12)	Mixed, Weak	1982	80	Promising	$146	$96
Roots and Wings (PreK–6)	Marginal	1993	200	Strong	$210	$70
School Development Program (K–12)	Promising	1968	700	Promising	$45	$32
Success for All (PreK–6)	Strong	1987	1130	Strong	$270	$70
Talent Development High School (9–12)	Marginal	1994	10	Strong	$57	$27
Urban Learning Centers (PreK–12)	?	1993	13	Promising	$169	$159

Costs are in thousands of dollars (e.g., $62=$62,000); NA = Not Available; NC = No change

The Accelerated Schools model developed by Levin was tremendously successful in turning around a school that had a long history of being the lowest-performing school in the district. The Core Knowledge model was used by a charter school and was very successful in producing high levels of achievement on both nationally-normed and criterion-referenced assessments. The Edison Schools model used both Success for All and Roots and Wings. We found both to be extremely effective in raising all ability achievement levels of students. Two other models being installed as this book is written include Ernest Boyer's Basic School model, which a traditional neighborhood school will be implementing, and the Expeditionary Learning Outward Bound model, which is being implemented by a charter school. According to *An Educators' Guide to Schoolwide Reform*, the Expeditionary model has been fairly successful in raising student achievement whereas the Basic School model has no track record. However, many of the elements described in Boyer's book *The Basic School* would lead one to believe that increased student achievement should accompany the model.

Regardless of the models that a school/district thinks are most promising, the whole-school reform models are another way of introducing competition through choice and thereby accelerating student achievement.

Restructure Traditional Schools

Big questions will emerge when a school district is engaged in introducing choice—whether it be through charter schools, private for-profits, magnets, schools-within-schools, or whole-school reform models. These questions are: "Is it necessary to restructure every school?" "Is the old, traditional neighborhood school a thing of the past?" "Are the new school models another fad in education that will go away in a few years?" It is my belief that neighborhood schools will remain the first choice of the majority of parents and students as long as the education the students are getting in those schools meets certain minimum expectations. Most parents will default to their neighborhood school because of the convenience factor alone. In addition, most parents want their children to play with, and be around, the children in their immediate neighborhood, and these are the children that go to the neighborhood school.

Although neighborhood schools will remain the first option of most parents, that does not mean that those schools should not be restructured to some degree. Even those schools that are successful and have high student achievement can get better and, therefore, must look to some of the models, or the components of the models, to improve. In addition, the success of choice schools will force change in the traditional neighborhood schools. However, resistance will come from those people who are satisfied with the traditional neighborhood-school design and who do not feel it is wise to change, especially if the change is radical in nature or if the change could be viewed as having more negative aspects than positive. Therefore, an impetus must be given to traditional schools whose staffs may be reluctant to restructure the school. There are many ways to provide such an impetus, but I next describe a method that we used in one of my districts that proved to be extremely successful.

Each elementary school was given a $20,000 planning grant that the principal and staff could use in any way they thought best. The funds could be used for release time for staff, consultants, travel, materials, training, or any other purpose that supported the school in examining the research and best practices being used throughout the country. They were given an entire year to complete their investigations and to develop a plan for how they wished to restructure or alter their school design. Assistance was provided through the district's academic achievement department to help in any manner the schools needed or requested. There was one primary and one secondary goal of any proposed restructuring. The primary goal was to increase student achievement and learning. To help assure this, research of the best practices would have to indicate that such a restructuring should lead to increased academic achievement. The secondary goal applied to schools whose student populations had sunk below 400, which we considered to be the minimum number necessary to efficiently operate an elementary school. Although the district was growing at a rate of about 500 students per year, some schools had lost student population for a number of reasons, including aging neighborhoods and the opening of choice schools within the district. The secondary goal was to have all schools operating in an efficient range of 400 to 650 students. A further financial incentive awaited schools upon the completion and approval of their restructuring plans. A permanent grant of $108,000 would go to non-Title I schools and $150,000 would go to Title I schools in order for them to implement the plans they had designed. These funds could be used for any purpose, including the employment of teaching and support staff.

Just as important as financial incentives were in encouraging staffs to look at ways they might be able to restructure their schools was the financial disincentive to those schools that continued to lose student population and that were operating with less than 400 students. Whenever the number of students dropped below 400, the school needed to make adjustments in staffing patterns because the funding formula used by the district naturally provided greater latitude to the principal in schools with more than 400 students. The number of students per class could stay the same, but the number of full-time teaching equivalents given to the school was insufficient to continue to provide full-time staff in support areas such as physical education, music, and art. Thus, those teachers had to assume other duties, relocate to another school, or accept less than a full-time position. Students continued to have the same amount of time in the affected areas; thus, there was no diminution of services to students. A movement among staff started that was designed to guarantee the same number of support positions when the student population dropped below 400. This was resisted by central administration because of the safety net it provided to schools. If a school was guaranteed to keep a minimum number of full-time teaching equivalents, there would be no incentive to restructure the school to attract more students from around the district. Thus, competition would have been effectively eliminated. This caused great angst within the district, but was necessary for true competition to exist.

The restructuring of our traditional elementary schools was a huge success. Every school closely examined the literature and studied the practices that were making a difference in student learning in other schools. Every school intensely reexamined its basic beliefs and determined the needs and desires of the community it served. Every school performed site visits to schools within and outside of the district to observe practices about which they had read. In the end, each made, or is in the process of making, significant shifts in the way they operated. Each school made unique decisions, but each of those decisions was a sound, deliberate decision that bolstered student achievement. One school was transforming itself into the district's second Primary Years Program International Baccalaureate school; another was adopting Boyer's Basic School model; another became an academy for math and science; another embraced the Accelerated School model; others moved to block scheduling that decreased pupil-teacher ratios in language arts and doubled teacher planning time; foreign language was instituted or planned to be instituted in every school; uninterrupted blocks of time for language arts and/or mathematics instruction was a common theme; common sequential curriculum and texts/materials became the norm with phonetic instruction included within a rich literature base; and expanded individual tutorial assistance was common in restructured schools.

It is my opinion that all traditional neighborhood schools must periodically reinvent themselves to become better. If a climate of cooperative competition exists in a district, such schools have an incentive to examine themselves and to change as they deem proper to better educate children and to improve student achievement.

5

Define the
Power Structure

Empower School Leaders

Most of the research on site-based management indicates that there is no increase in student achievement when it is implemented. In my opinion, that is because it has not been implemented properly. If done correctly, site-based management can be a significant factor in raising student achievement.

Everyone wants to have control of his or her life. All people want to feel as if they determine what happens to them. No one wants to feel manipulated or powerless. In today's world the feeling of powerlessness is perhaps greater than it has ever been. Companies downsize or reorganize on a regular basis, and for most people who work for a company, little can be done to affect the change. They simply must accept the new structure and their places in the new organizational environment. A rapidly changing economy often affects us as individuals, and we are absolutely powerless to escape the effects. Politicians pass laws that affect our personal and professional lives. This has been particularly true for educators during the last decade because state legislatures increasingly feel obligated to pass laws that effect public schools. For example, with the passage of charter-school legislation in a state, the lives of educators are forever changed, and, for the most part, individual educators are powerless to alter their destiny.

Even changes in the simple facets in our lives make us feel powerless. Whenever the cable or satellite television company decides to change all of the channel numbers that had previously been assigned to stations, our lives are changed. We must unlearn all of the old numbers and remember all of the new ones. We have no choice in the matter. We are powerless in the matter. When we get a notice from our car manufacturer that a defect has been detected in the year and model of an automobile we own, we must take it back to the dealer for repair. We do not have the time to devote to do this, but we have no real choice. If we want the defect fixed, we must take the car to the shop. There are countless examples in our everyday lives of our powerlessness. It is this general feeling of powerlessness that makes it vitally important for us to feel that we have some control over the major aspects of our lives; one of the most important of those is our work. We want to feel as if we are empowered to effect changes in our jobs. This is just as true for educators as it is for other professions. We are happier individuals, and we tend to put more time, energy, and effort into our work when we feel empowered.

These thoughts are shared by Charles Schwahn and William Spady in their book *Total Leaders*. They phrase it this way:

> *Empowered people produce.* Empowering qualified people to have more control over their work is morally right and profitable. Empowerment honors the intrinsic motivation of people to use their expertise to best advantage and gives them a direct stake in achieving personal and organizational success. Empowerment works best when employees deeply identify with organizational purpose, have a clear vision of where the organization wants to go, have a strong commitment to getting there, and receive the necessary organizational supports.

Empowerment is the correct approach to improving schools and student achievement, but it must be done properly to get the desired results.

Determine the Final
Authority for All Decision Points

There are many different methods of empowering individuals in an organization or of operating site-based managed systems. Almost any technique or system will work as long as all parties involved adhere to the ultimate mission of the district. However, it is critical for some decisions to be retained at upper levels within the district as a check and balance on the majority of decisions, which should be vested in the school site. In essence, site-based management will work to increase student achievement only if the site and district work in an overall system designed for that purpose. We have already seen that individuals will act in their own best interests when it comes to proposed changes for a school/district. If all authority is vested in the school, the individuals within that school will not act in the best interests of students unless it coincides with their own best interests. This is human nature, is quite normal, and will occur unless there is some counterbalance. This counterbalance is the district central office, which can act more objectively in some matters than school personnel simply because the central office has no vested interest in the operation of the school except to see increased student achievement. Thus, each district or each board of education needs to determine exactly where the final authority rests for the various major decision points within the operation of a school district.

The way that we accomplished this in two of my districts was to develop a site-based management/shared decision-making matrix that was formally approved by the board of education. The step of having the board approve the matrix is extremely important. In most states, it is the board that has complete legal authority over a district. Consequently, it is critical that the board understands and agrees to give away the power to make certain decisions without later questioning those decisions if they run counter to the board members' own thinking. Just as important, any unions operating in the district must cede away authority they have accrued through negotiated contracts that run counter to site-based management. The chart beginning on the next page is an example of a decision matrix for determining who has authority for specific decisions.

Each school district or board of education will ascertain that various decisions should rest at various places within the organization. The matrix presented on the next page is not the perfect matrix. There is no perfect matrix. It will vary from district to district depending on the vagaries and peculiarities of the district. For example, in the sample matrix, the board of education insisted on retaining the right to make the final decision of the choice of colors and logos of new schools being built for the district. This is obvious micromanagement of an unimportant decision and is best left to the school to decide. However, for this board and the nature of the district, the board members felt it was important enough for them to retain the right to make the final decision on such a trivial matter.

It is also important to note that although the final decisions rest at specific levels, the expectation is that all stakeholder groups that would be affected by a decision have a right to be involved to some degree in making recommendations to the ultimate decision maker. For example, in the instance where the board retained final authority of a new school's choice of colors or logo, the school itself should certainly provide the initial recommendations to the board, which should then take the recommendations into consideration before making a final decision. It is also important to note that whereas all stakeholder groups should be involved in making recommendations, not all stakeholders will have that opportunity. Many school districts are simply too large to afford the opportunity for all individuals to be directly involved in decisions. Thus, the involvement is representational and not direct.

(Text continues on page 152.)

Site-Based Management/
Shared Decision-Making Matrix

When making decisions, sites shall solicit input from members of each group affected by a particular decision, including students, teachers, site staff, parents, business leaders, and community representatives. This input will be taken into consideration as decisions are made.

An "X" in the matrix reflects where the final decision will be made or the office with the final authority.

	Site	Central Office	Board of Education
Assessment—Districtwide		AA	
Assessment—Site	X		
Budget—District			X
Budget—School	X		
Building Accountability		S	
Calendar			X
Choice Schools/Programs			X
Cocurricular Programs	X		
Course Offerings		AA	
Curriculum:			
Grading Scale	X		
Library Materials	X		
Master Schedule	X		
Methodology	X		
Scope and Sequence		AA	
Content Standards		AA	
Performance Standards		AA	
Textbook Selection	X		
Custodial Services		BS	
Day Start/Stop Time		T	
District Goals			X

	Site	Central Office	Board of Education
District Mission			X
District Philosophy			X
Emergency Closings		BS	
Employee Benefits:			
Funding			X
Selection		HR	
Employment/Termination:			
Administrator		S	
Certified	X		
Classified	X		
Superintendent			X
Enrollment		HR	
Evaluation:			
Administrator		S	
Certified	X		
Classified	X		
Superintendent			X
Facilities:			
Boundaries		BS	
Building Design			X
Construction		FAC	
Energy Management		FAC	
Maintenance		FAC	
Food Service		FS	
Grade Requirements:			
Weighted System	X		
Assigning Letter Grades			X
Graduation Requirements			X

	Site	Central Office	Board of Education
Homework Requirements		AA	
Grants		AA	
Length of School Day			X
Length of School Year			X
Policies			X
Purchasing:			
Bid		P	
Selection	X		
School Colors and Logo			X
School Name			X
Staffing Allocation		HR	
Staffing Design	X		
Staff Development—District		AA	
Staff Development—School	X		
Students:			
Behavior Standards	X		
Detention	X		
Discipline	X		
Dress Code	X		
Expulsion		S	
Substitutes:			
Establishing Pool		HR	
Selection	X		
Technology:			
Hardware		TECH	
System Software		TECH	
Software	X		
Time Spent on Core Subjects			X

	Site	Central Office	Board of Education
Transfers		HR	
Transportation:			
Pick Up/Drop Off		T	
Establish Routes		T	

AA—Academic Achievement; BS—Business Services; FAC—Facilities; FS—Food Service; HR—Human Resources; P—Purchasing; S—Superintendent; T—Transportation; TECH—Technology

Of the 70 decision points listed in the matrix, only four (less than 6 percent) rested with me as the superintendent. There is a reason for this. Just as it is important for the board of education and the unions to cede power, it is important that the superintendent do the same. Unless it is critical to maintain the district's mission of increased student achievement, a decision point should rest someplace other than with the superintendent. It is also highly symbolic for a superintendent to vest authority to others. After all, in developing a district decision-making matrix, the superintendent is asking the board and unions to give away power in some instances. It is only fitting that the superintendent does the same.

Even though I retained only four decision points, it is critical to note which points were retained. They were: building accountability, administrator employment and termination, administrator evaluation, and student expulsion. The student expulsion decisions were a matter of administrative convenience because of the size of the district. The board had to be removed from having to attend a large number of hearings to make expulsion decisions. This was much better handled by my executive assistant, who acted as the judge on such cases.

However, the first three decision points were intentionally retained at the superintendent level to provide the necessary check and balance to keep the district on course with its mission. Building accountability was the policy that was put in place to assure that schools and principals were aligned with the district's mission and philosophy, and that they would be held accountable for student achievement. Whenever the size of the district permits, the superintendent should be directly involved with establishing those expectations and monitoring whether the goals established for the school are being met. The other two decision points are also critical to the success of the district and to assure increased student achievement. The superintendent must retain the right to hire leaders who have a philosophy consistent with the district's mission and philosophy and who have the skills necessary to have others follow them in the direction the district wishes to go. Just as important, the superintendent must retain the final authority as to which administrators must be terminated. Finally, the superintendent must be directly involved in, and have the final authority for, the evaluation of administrators.

Once a decision matrix has been developed for the district, each school must then develop a matrix for the school that clearly indicates who will have the final authority to make decisions that are vested in the school site. In thesample decision matrix, more than 31 percent of all decisions were given to schools. Just as it is important to have a clear delineation as to who has what authority at the district level, it is important to have the same type of delineation at the school site—for example, who will retain the final decision as to which textbooks are used in a course or subject. This can be done in any number of ways, from total shared decision making, where consensus must be reached from department or grade level teams, to recommendations being made to the principal who holds the final authority. The development of the matrix is truly left up to each school site, but the matrix must be completed and must be done in an unambiguous manner.

Finally, it is important for a district to have a process in place that enables waivers from the district decision matrix to be given to a school. The school should be required to put forth a cogent argument, backed by research, that indicates that student achievement should increase if something different is done. For example, in the matrix, the board of education retained the right to determine the length of the school day. This right is necessary to prevent a school from shortening the school day, which runs counter to what research indicates will lead to increased student achievement. However, there are more and more schools where the leaders understand the importance of time on task and wish to increase the school day to increase student achievement. A process must be in place in a district that enables, and even encourages, such waiver requests. The same can be said for the scope and sequence of the curriculum. Schools should have great latitude in curriculum matters as long as they adhere to state or district standards. However, a scope-and-sequence can be done in a variety of ways and still conform to the district's overall standards. A process should be in place that would enable a school to alter the sequence of the curriculum as long as it can show that the scope will be maintained over time. In addition, schools may wish to add various items to the curriculum and should be empowered to do so as long as they can demonstrate that the required standards will be met.

Change the Funding Mechanism

Although it has been in vogue for the past decade to talk about empowering schools, the truth is that in most cases true empowerment has not occurred. Educators have merely nibbled around the edges of empowerment. The central offices of school districts still control the vast majority of funds that go to schools. I argued for the need to provide greater staffing flexibility to schools in an article published in the April 1991 issue of *The School Administrator*. Since that time, many districts have switched to a staffing formula that permits schools to utilize staff in a variety of ways instead of in a prescribed fashion. I now realize that as empowering as that suggestion was, it did not go far enough in advocating for greater flexibility for schools.

The reason I claim that schools are not as empowered as they should be is because districts have not given schools the very essence of power—money. Only when a school controls all of the money necessary to operate the school does true empowerment occur. As long as people situated outside of the school determine how funds can and cannot be used, schools will not be empowered to the degree that is necessary for dramatic changes to take effect and for student achievement to soar. It is for this reason that we undertook to fund schools differently in one of my districts.

We had recently had our first charter school apply for approval from the district. Charters were required to be funded by the state at a minimum of 80 percent of the Per Pupil Operating Revenue (PPOR) determined for that district by the state. The state later changed this requirement to 95 percent. The charter could utilize the funds in any manner it wished. The advantages to this are enormous. Funds that would ordinarily be spent on operating the school that could be saved through some cost-cutting measure could then be retained at the school and expended on other, higher-priority items. For example, a charter could determine that transportation would not be provided and that parents would have to find other ways to get their children to school, e.g., public transportation, car pooling, etc. The funds that would have ordinarily been spent on transportation could then be spent on such items as lower class size. Thus, an incentive was provided to schools to determine their priorities and to budget accordingly.

We decided to fund some of our regular, noncharter schools in the same manner. We started with just three elementary schools. We got exactly what we expected. The schools used savings in a variety of areas to provide programs they ordinarily would not have been able to provide. Although many district principals looked askance at this funding mechanism, we continued to expand it to other schools. We were by no means the first school district to fund schools in this manner. There are a number of districts around North America that utilize this funding mechanism. Perhaps the most experienced district with the most extensive and most detailed system is Edmonton, Canada. However, there are still very few districts that do empower their schools in this manner.

The largest single advantage of a PPOR funding mechanism is the control and incentive it gives a school over the single highest expense of operating a school—labor costs. Normally, a school district expends 80 to 85 percent of its total operating revenue on salary and benefits. This is not unusual in a service-oriented industry, but it is higher than necessary and takes valuable resources away from other areas of the budget. Most school districts operate under a negotiated or board-approved salary schedule(s) that is usually based on degrees and experience. The amount of money paid to a new hire depends strictly on where they fit on the salary schedule. Normally, no restrictions are put on a school as to how much money it can expend on salaries and benefits. The schools simply interview the available applicants and employ whom they consider to be a quality candidate regardless of the salary the individual will receive. There is absolutely no incentive to control the total amount of funds expended for labor. Indeed, the opposite is often true, with schools being positively recognized and acclaimed for the percentage of staff that have advanced degrees and extensive experience.

Imagine a business designing a system that cannot control labor costs. Imagine a business that pays no attention to the availability of trained personnel in the labor force. Imagine a business where each of the subunits has no concern about the amount that it spends on salaries and benefits. It would be out of business in a short time. Well, that is exactly the system that public education has designed and it is one that must be fixed if sufficient funds are ever to be available to educate all children to the degree we can.

In a PPOR funding arrangement, each school is responsible for all of its costs, including labor. This introduces a tremendous opportunity to such schools. Every dollar they can save on labor costs can be spent in any way the school sees fit, including additional labor. Instead of employing people regardless of their degree and experience, schools would employ people who are quality teachers but who are not necessarily the most costly. There are many quality teachers available who do not hold advanced degrees or training, or who do not possess maximum experience. I know this as a fact after many years of interviewing and employing literally thousands of teachers. There is some truth to the old saying that after three years of teaching experience, more experience does not automatically make one a better teacher. Once a certain degree of competence is reached through experience, additional experience will not automatically add to competence. The same can be said of obtaining additional degrees from our teacher education institutions. All too often, an advanced degree does not prepare one to be a better teacher. This, of course, is not always the case, but a valid argument can be made that advanced degrees do not necessarily make for better results.

An example of how employing quality people while keeping an eye on the bottom line—which can be a benefit to schools—helps bring the power of the PPOR funding mechanism into focus. My example is a school of 500 students that has an average of 25 students per class. This gives the school 20 regular classroom teachers. The salary for the district's teacher salary schedule ranges from $27,000 to $57,000. It costs an additional 25 percent per teacher for employee benefits, making the total cost per teacher range from $33,750 to $71,250. The school has three openings for the coming year. Two of the teachers are veterans who are retiring, and the other is a mid-career teacher whose spouse has taken a position that forces a move. The average cost of these three teachers is $60,000, for a total labor cost of $180,000. A number of quality applicants are available. Instead of employing individuals who have comparable degrees/training and experience, the school employs teachers they believe are quality instructors but with fewer degrees/training and less experience. One of them is even a beginning teacher who did her student teaching at the school and was very successful. The average cost for the three new teachers is $42,000 for a total of $126,000 or a savings of $54,000. In a PPOR school, the school retains this $54,000, which can then be spent in other areas. The school decides it would like to have a reading teacher that it does not currently have. It interviews and employees a teacher who costs $46,000. The school still has savings of $8,000 for future use and has obtained a reading specialist it never had before.

The biggest critics of PPOR schools will, of course, be teacher/employee unions. The primary argument is that schools will employ "less qualified" people and achievement will fall. There is no doubt that schools would employ "less qualified" people but, as previously explained, "less qualified" does not equate to less competent. Therefore, "less qualified" staff members do not mean that students will suffer. Indeed, the exact opposite will occur because schools will have more funds available to enhance the learning of students.

I have also heard the argument that schools that watch the bottom line of labor costs will never employ highly trained and experienced teachers. This was not the case in my school district. What we experienced was simply a better mix of training and experience in schools. Most principals will openly share that they prefer to have a staff with various degrees of training and experience as well as various skills and expertise. A school does not need everyone to be highly skilled in all areas. All staff need to be highly skilled only in specific critical areas. For example, all elementary teachers should be experts in teaching reading, writing, and mathematics. They do not need to be experts in social studies, or the sciences, or art, or music. All high-school teachers need to be experts in student discipline, but not in all content areas—not even in all areas in their specific field. A science teacher, for example, may specialize in biology and not be technically proficient in physics as long as she is not required to teach physics. The same is true for degrees and experience. A much better mix exists if a school has a blend of teachers with varying amounts of training and experience. Young, inexperienced teachers can be mentored by older, more experienced staff. Older, less newly trained teachers can learn new methods taught to the younger, more recently trained teachers by their teacher training institutions. A department full of younger teachers would profit greatly from a more highly trained, experienced teacher. Thus, there will be times when schools intentionally seek out such teachers, just as there will be times when they seek the opposite.

No doubt, awareness training will need to be provided to teachers and staff before the benefits of a PPOR funding model will be fully understood and realized. There is also no doubt that principals who have been trained as instructional leaders will need training in budgeting and cost-control management skills to be able to fully utilize the benefits of a PPOR funding mechanism. Until that training is provided, many of the very people who stand to gain the most from the model, the principals, may resist. However, with sufficient training and support, I am convinced that most will welcome the concept because of the empowerment that it gives to the schools. It is a powerful tool to help schools improve student performance.

6

Implement Traditional Achievement Factors

There are a number of other factors that seem to have a mild to strong positive correlation to student achievement that have been much discussed, debated, and written about for the last 20 to 30 years. Virtually all of these factors have been researched extensively. They are often the focus of school/district improvement efforts and have been implemented in part or in whole in various schools/districts across the country. However, almost all of these factors are extremely expensive, and this expense has severely hampered their implementation in a wholesale manner. Indeed, for those states, districts, and schools that have tried to implement some of these factors, the expense has caused only a partial implementation that has most often resulted in the factor's effectiveness being mostly or completely lost. For example, lowering class size may well be able to improve achievement, but most of the research indicates that significant positive results occur only when class size has been lowered to a level that would bankrupt the schools/districts. The same can be said about preschool programs, increasing teacher pay to attract and retain quality teachers, ongoing and thorough staff development, and creating smaller schools.

Others factors, like many of the elements discussed in previous sections of this book, are highly political in nature and are, therefore, rife with contention. This has often resulted in these factors not being implemented in a widespread fashion. For example, switching the starting times of elementary and secondary schools probably makes good sense from an achievement point of view, but the negating affect this switch would have on most of the current high-school after-school activities makes it difficult or impossible to implement in most localities.

Nonetheless, these more traditional achievement factors should be considered as a part an overall effort a school/district can use to increase student performance. However, one important point needs to be made. These traditional factors cannot replace the essential elements that make up the bulk of this book. Indeed, personal experience has taught me that significant and dramatic student achievement gains can be made without most of these more traditional achievement factors. It would be a grave error to continue to exclusively or predominately emphasize these traditional factors. They simply are not going to happen, and even if they did, I am convinced that they cannot, in and of themselves, dramatically improve student achievement. That being said, they are important, and at least one is essential, if schools/districts are to have a major impact on improving student performance.

Employ and Retain Quality Teachers

We have innately known for many years that the quality of a teacher makes a difference in how much students learn. However, there has been a paucity of objective data to support what we thought to be true until just recently. The most startling data come from William Sanders and the Tennessee Value-Added Research and Assessment Center. His research has led to a number of rather impressive findings. He bases these findings on a large, longitudinal database that links student achievement results to schools and individual teachers as the students moved from grade to grade. He has concluded:

♦ There is no way to accurately predict student achievement based on the social-economic make-up of the community that feeds the school.

♦ Student achievement is not related to racial composition.

♦ The socioeconomic level of the students does not determine student achievement levels.

♦ The most important determiner of student achievement is teacher effectiveness.

♦ Gifted students grow less academically from year to year than do lower-achieving students.

♦ Student academic growth occurs in spurts and plateaus.

♦ When the majority of students in a class show either an academic spurt or plateau, teacher effectiveness is the reason.

♦ An individual teacher's effectiveness tends to remain the same from year to year when he/she moves to a different school.

♦ Even when an effective teacher moves from a high-performing school to a low-performing school, that teacher's students continue to have high levels of academic achievement.

♦ Students who have had ineffective teachers continue to have the negative residual effects of low achievement for many years thereafter, even when they have effective teachers in later years.

Dr. Sanders' research is very powerful. It not only confirms the importance of employing and retaining quality teachers, but it also reinforces the notion that any school and any school district can have high academic achievement. The old belief that students who receive free or reduced-price lunches cannot achieve at high levels has been brought into serious question by Sanders' work.

An article in the April 1998 issue of *The American School Board Journal* points out other data supporting the long-held belief that the quality of the teacher makes a difference in student learning. It cites a study done at the University of Tennessee 15 years ago that showed that the difference in the quality of teachers accounted for as much as 50 to 60 percentile points on standardized tests. It also cites a Texas study, *Doing What Matters Most: Investing in Quality Teaching,* done by the state's teachers commission that shows the effects of teaching are "so strong, and the variations in teacher expertise so great that, after controlling for socioeconomic status, the large disparities between black and white students were almost entirely accounted for by differences in the qualifications of their teachers." The same article also cites Linda Darling-Hammond, executive director of the National Commission on Teaching and America's Future, as stating that the commission "determined that the single-most important determinant of how students achieve is their teachers' qualifications." She further stated that the absence of proper credentials has a negative effect on student achievement and that a master's degree has little or no effect, but scores on state teacher licensing examinations "have a very large effect on student achievement."

Although the importance of teacher quality cannot, and should not, be discounted or lessened, it is important to remember that a teacher can only do so much to assist students to achieve. There are other, vitally important factors that must be present if students are to achieve to their maximum capability. To illustrate this point, I will compare a teacher in a school to a pilot in a plane. A pilot is the most important ingredient in successfully flying a plane from New York to London. Without a trained pilot, the plane will never leave the ground, fly between two specific destinations, and land safely. However, how well a pilot can perform his job depends on the design of the airplane. The plane could be a project or the Concorde. Both will get passengers from New York to London, but one will get them there much quicker. The plane could be a small jet that holds 20 passengers or it could be a jumbo jet that holds 240. The pilot of the small jet could transport all 240 people the jumbo jet holds, but it would take 12 trips to accomplish the same thing the jumbo jet could do in just one. The cockpit of a larger plane may accommodate the pilot and two copilots, whereas a smaller plane seats the pilot and only one copilot, even though both planes have the same safety record. The second plane will do the same job as the first, but less expensively, thus providing for lower ticket prices or more profit for the airline. One plane may have Doppler radar that can detect wind shear whereas another does not. The first plane can, therefore, avoid potentially deadly storms, whereas the other cannot.

Teachers in a school are in a similar situation. They can successfully teach the students who are assigned to them, but they can do a much better job if the school is designed for maximum effectiveness. For example, if the school follows a block schedule that gives the teacher two and one half hours of uninterrupted time for language arts, the teacher can be more effective than if the school permits students to be pulled during that time for various activities. The entire faculty can be more effective if they have all agreed upon a commonly used curriculum, texts, and materials that articulate what each teacher is responsible to teach than if individual teachers develop their own curriculum and utilize different textbooks and materials. Teachers can be more effective and their students can learn more if the school year is 20 days longer, or if the school day is an hour longer. Students will learn to some degree without these elements in the school's design, but they will learn more if they are present. Thus, it is vital to wed effective teachers with effective design if students are to reach their full potential.

Create and Maintain Student Discipline, Mutual Respect, and School Order

It should be self-evident to most observers that learning will not occur in a school unless the school provides a safe, supportive, and disciplined environment. Along with quality teachers, such an environment is perhaps one of the most important factors in securing or advancing student achievement. For schools that are currently "out of control," the first step to take in increasing student performance is to establish adequate discipline. Even for schools that have moderate discipline, achievement can be quickly enhanced by creating what I call a "culture of order." Such a culture is one that honors and respects the rights and privileges of others by setting clearly defined behavioral expectations that are easily understood by students.

Although it is difficult to describe such a culture, one can immediately tell when first entering the front door whether a school has it or not. A culture of order does not need to be one where quiet is demanded or one where uniformity is required or one with the proverbial gallows by the front door. It does, however, have to be one where adults, and not students, control the environment. However, student involvement in such matters as casting the rules and dispensing consequences through a student court, or voting to decide what the school uniforms should look like, can be the rule. Despite the serious involvement of students, it is the adults who must remain in control and the adults who establish the limits or boundaries of acceptable behavior. This essential requirement is not meant to establish an environment in which students are dominated by adults, but is a simple recognition that students are children and adolescents who have not yet fully established their moral or ethical code and who have not yet had the life experiences necessary to always know the borderline between acceptable behavior and behavior that can easily become harmful to themselves or others.

What are some of the ways that schools can create and maintain a culture of order? I list below a few of the more prominent methods used by schools and districts that have such cultures. Not all of the factors need to be present to have a safe and secure learning environment. Each school and each district is unique and must determine what works best for it, but all of the factors positively affect the school climate and, consequently, help to increase student performance.

◆ **School uniforms**

Much has been written on the possible positive effects that uniforms have on helping to create order and discipline. Most schools that require a uniform give anecdotal reports of lessened school violence, greater student respect for themselves and others, and fewer violations of the school rules. Although there will invariably be differences of opinion on whether or not a school should require a uniform, this is a fairly easy and quick way to improve school discipline if behavior in the school is interfering with learning.

♦ **Zero tolerance**

Once again we encounter a policy where there is no universal agreement as to whether or not a district should establish a policy whereby students are suspended or expelled for the first offense involving drugs or violence. Many people argue that latitude should be given to school and district administrators regarding the disposition of such offenses. The popular media certainly has a field day whenever a student, especially a young student, is required to be suspended or expelled for what appears to be a minor or accidental offense. In addition, some people have asserted that statistics do not indicate that drug or violent offenses have decreased as a result of zero tolerance. To date, I have not found any convincing or conclusive evidence that such acts either increase or decrease as a result of zero tolerance policies or the absence of those policies. Therefore, I have only my personal experience upon which to rely.

I have instituted zero-tolerance policies in two school districts in which I served as superintendent. In both instances, the district and I were taken to court for allegedly violating the constitutional rights of the students to a public education because of the severity of an automatic yearlong expulsion. The students' attorneys claimed that the expulsions were arbitrary and did not fit the level of the offense. In both cases the students were in middle school. One case involved the bringing of an antique but operable gun to school, and the other involved an attempt to sell a hallucinogenic mushroom at school. Both cases were rather long and protracted, and both cases garnered a good deal of publicity. The school district won both cases. Although neither of these cases was pleasant, and although both involved personal verbal attacks on me by the two judges, they were well worth the time, effort, and expense. I am convinced that the zero-tolerance policies set a clear standard by which students in the districts were expected to abide as well as establishing a clear consequence for a violation of the standard. As a result, there were far fewer cases of violence or drugs on the campuses than there had been prior to the adoption of the policies. Consequently, I strongly encourage any school or district that wishes to have a culture of order to adopt zero-tolerance policies for drugs and violence.

♦ Nurturing adults

Along with policies that establish consequences for inappropriate actions, a school needs to strive to become a place that nurtures the young people who are there. To some, this may seem like a contradiction but it really is not. Children and adolescents need to know that they are loved and respected just as they need to know that there are boundaries with consequences for crossing those boundaries.

♦ Limited rules

From a review of the literature, it appears that though there need to be clearly established rules for a school, those rules need to be relatively few in number. Apparently, a more exhaustive list of rules makes students feel more like inmates than students and can actually do more harm than good in attempting to create a culture of order. No magic number has been determined, but more than five or six seems to be an area where more general rules start to become more specialized and less effective.

♦ School-wide rules

One surefire way to develop resentment, confusion, and a desire to rebel is for teachers in a school to establish their own rules instead of having one set of rules that applies to all students at all times in all places. The reasoning is simple. Rules are more easily remembered and easier for students to apply when they are universal in nature and not subject to the peculiarities of individual teachers.

♦ School-wide values

Once upon a time, not too long ago, whenever one would mention values education the ears of the conservative right would perk up and a battle would ensue between those in public education who wanted to teach values to public school children and parents who wanted to exclusively teach their children the values they thought were important. Those battles are pretty much behind us because those on all sides of the issue now concur that regardless of their own personal religious, political, or ethnic background, the vast majority of people can agree on a few select values that should be taught to our young people. It is not difficult to get even the most contentious group of people to agree that honesty is generally a good thing or that stealing is a bad thing. Schools or districts with a culture of order generally are ones that have engaged their communities and commonly agreed upon a few values that can, and should, make up the foundation of the schools or districts themselves and that are routinely and systemically taught to its young people.

Of course, there are many other ways of establishing and maintaining discipline and respect in a school or district. Teachers have to be knowledgeable in, and expert at, behavioral controls for the classroom; administrators need to be consistent in assigning consequences; teachers need to be supported whenever possible for decisions they make regarding classroom discipline; and all adults must be in the hallways before and after school, and between classes and in the cafeteria at lunch. The important thing to note is simply that a culture of order must exist if learning is to occur for students. Create and maintain it, and student performance will rise as a result.

Upgrade Skills Through Ongoing and Frequent Staff Development

A corollary to employing and retaining quality teachers is providing ongoing and frequent staff development for those very same teachers. We know that staff development makes eminent sense. Indeed, virtually no one will disagree. The problem comes when you must provide time and funds for the staff development. Then, it becomes a problem. That is why Allan Odden even recommends eliminating a noncore curriculum area such as physical education, art, or music and taking the funds saved and putting them into yearly staff development. I worked for 27 years as an administrator in a number of public school districts and the effort to get adequate funds for staff development was an ongoing struggle that never ended. My experiences are no different from those of most public-school educators. In one district, I could not convince the board of education that staff development should be a critical piece of a long-range strategic plan that we were developing at the time. The 125 community members that served on the task force understood and supported the idea, but the board voted to keep it in a low tier of funding priorities. Private business routinely spends 5 to 10 percent of its annual operating budget on developing its staff to perform their job functions. School districts consider themselves lucky to expend 0.5 percent on its teachers and staff. Regardless of how the funds are obtained, they are critical for increased student achievement.

Not only are funds necessary, but the manner in which the staff development is delivered is also important. For three decades, I have witnessed arguments as to what is the best method of developing staff. In one of my districts, we developed a system whereby teachers designed their own staff development. They decided in which areas they could improve and then sought out ways to get trained in that area. This approach has its advantages and does improve the ability of individual teachers. However, if staff development is limited to this approach, a critical element is missing. There are times when a school/district should decide that it must emphasize a particular subject, method, or area that most teachers would not choose for staff development if the decision were left entirely up to each teacher. A number of personal examples will illustrate the point. When one state developed and required state standards for the first time, staff needed training in how to alter their instruction to teach the new standards. In another district, the middle-school administrators determined that to increase student achievement in reading, everyone in the schools would be required to teach reading every day. This required training teachers who were not language arts instructors. A third example occurred in two districts where a decision was made to use the Six-Trait Writing Assessment as the methodology to be used to assess writing. Everyone in the district needed to receive training in Six Traits. All of these examples required necessary training that a number of people initially resisted. By the way, all resulted in significantly increased student achievement.

The best of all models is a combination of staff development determined by individual teachers and district-required staff development. In one of my districts, each school was charged to examine its strengths and weaknesses as they applied to student achievement, to review the literature and research, and to restructure the school based on its own self-examination. As a part of this effort, it was incumbent on each school to determine how staff would be trained to implement the restructuring. Thus, each school had a common charge, but each was allowed to pursue it in the manner the professionals in the school thought best, including the training that they felt was necessary.

In reality, a mix of individual-teacher-determined staff development and a commonly agreed upon or school/district-imposed staff development is needed in our public schools. There are some staff development efforts that simply require everyone to be involved and to be trained. At other times, a small team of teachers, such as the math department at a high school or a group of third-grade teachers, will best be able to determine the nature of the staff development they need. Finally, all teachers have some individual weaknesses that they wish to improve and that they can effectively pursue without the involvement of any other staff member.

Involve Parents

Studies have been done that indicate that the single strongest factor that correlates to student achievement is parental involvement. The National Coalition for Parental Involvement in Education certainly concludes that the benefits of parental involvement are enormous and extend well beyond student improvement. They note five main areas of benefit:

1. Students do better in school and in life. They are more likely to earn higher grades and test scores, graduate from high school, and go on to higher

education. Low-income and minority students benefit the most.

2. Parents become empowered. Parents develop confidence by helping their children learn at home. Many go on to further their own education and become active in the community.

3. Teacher morale improves. Teachers who work with families expect more from students and feel a stronger connection to, and support from, the community.

4. Schools get better. When parents are involved at home and at school, in ways that make them full partners, the performance of all children in the school tends to improve.

5. Communities grow stronger. Families feel more invested in the school system, and the school system becomes more responsive to parent and community needs.

Bob Chase, president of the National Education Association, provided a startling supportive statistic in a recent speech to the National Press Club in which he exhorted schools and districts to make it possible for teachers to reach out and go to parents who are simply too pressed for time to get to the school. Chase remarked, " … the reading and math scores of low-achieving students rose 40 to 50 percent between the third and fifth grade when teachers reached out to families throughout the school year, and not just when a child was in trouble."

Because parental involvement is apparently such a key to improved student achievement, any school or district that wants to increase student achievement should assess its strengths and weaknesses in this critical area, and then take deliberate and aggressive steps to increase the involvement of parents in the schools.

Lower the Class Size

Of all of the issues surrounding education, the one most supported by the lay public is the need to lower the class size. Parents and the general public have been convinced for decades that children learn more and learn more quickly when the class size is small. Teachers have concurred with this assessment. Indeed, there seems little question that teachers have been the primary source of initiating and maintaining this belief. It seems to make logical sense. The more students in the classroom, the less time the teacher can spend individually with each child and the greater the likelihood of off-task behavior that results in decreased learning, at best, and increased behavioral problems concomitant with decreased learning, at worst. Anyone who has been in a classroom with 30 students knows that it is difficult to even walk around the room because the desks are so crammed together. Private schools, and more recently, charter schools, have advertised low class sizes as a drawing card. It is clear that the association between student achievement and class size is deeply rooted in this country.

However, the linkage between achievement and class size is not so clear when the research is examined. The issue has become even cloudier in recent years. For years, meta-analyses of class-size studies indicated that there was no correlation between class size and student achievement. Some studies got better results with small class sizes whereas others did not. There did appear to be some linkage in student achievement and class size when class sizes were significantly lowered, but a minor reduction in class size did not increase student achievement. It appeared that to get measurable results, class sizes had to shrink to around 15 to 17. The problem, of course, was money. Very few school districts could afford to reduce class sizes that low. Verification that reduced class sizes could produce higher student performance came from the Tennessee Student/Teacher Achievement Ratio (STAR) study. STAR was the first comprehensive, longitudinal study of class size. It found that children in small classes of approximately 15 students had higher achievement than students in regular-size classes of approximately 25 students. The differences were significant, and they lasted years later, even when the students were returned to regular-size classes. Students from the smaller classes while in K–3 had better high-school graduation rates, higher grade point averages, and pursued post-secondary education at higher rates.

Harold Wenglinsky, of Educational Testing Service (ETS), obtained similar results when he studied achievement in mathematics of fourth graders. What he found was that inner-city students who were in small classes of fewer than 20 achieved about three-fourths of a grade level higher than students in classes larger than 20, whereas suburban students in smaller classes achieved about one-third of a grade level higher.

Then came California's class-size reduction effort in the late 1990s. With legislation mandating low class sizes in K–3, California made a major move to increase student achievement through lower class sizes in the primary grades. The early results were the exact opposite. Student achievement actually decreased. Supporters of lower class sizes have attributed the decrease in student performance to the lack of trained teachers. Literally thousands of qualified teachers were needed, all at the same time. Such large numbers were not available, which resulted in the employment of unqualified, untrained teachers. Making matters even worse was the flight of many inner-city teachers to the higher-paying suburbs with easier working conditions that suddenly had numerous openings. The final verdict on California's initiative is still out, as is the linkage between lower class size and student achievement. Even with data to support lower class size, most states will not be forthcoming with the necessary funds to significantly lower the pupil-teacher ratio. However, other methods, such as block scheduling and the use of all staff in a building to teach selected subjects, have been devised and can significantly lower class sizes in the critical core academic areas of language arts and mathematics. Programs such as *Success for All* utilized by thousands of schools throughout the country, have proven that such methods work and that student achievement can be increased, even without significant new levels of funding from wary state legislatures.

Begin a Preschool Program

Most researchers of student achievement agree that one highly successful method of increasing student performance is to provide early learning opportunities for children. Everything seems to point to the importance of early intervention. The brain research clearly shows that critical brain development and brain patterns occur early in life—literally starting in the womb and accelerating during the first two years of a baby's life. Although much has already been determined by the time a child is two, there continues to be a lot of development during the critical ages of three to five. Some people argue that fully half of children's school achievement is attributable to their home backgrounds and the kind of early learning opportunities they have had. In addition, considerable research is available that verifies that the more learning opportunities available to children during the early years, the greater the achievement of children when they reach first grade.

In a review of the literature conducted by *The American School Board Journal*, a number of programs stood out as shining examples of successful preschool programs and the effect they can have on student achievement. They concluded that the earlier a school/district could start working with children and their parents, the better. An example is Parents as Teachers (PAT), a national program housed in St. Louis that recruits parents in the maternity wards and provides training to the parents throughout the child's first three years. The program is so successful that since 1985 the state of Missouri has required all school districts to offer the program. Another example of a massive state initiative is South Carolina's First Steps program. This is a childhood initiative that is designed to assure that all children are able to enter first grade both healthy and with sufficient readiness preschool activities to make them ready to learn typical first-grade materials. Each of the state's counties has a community board that determines how best to spend the money provided by the state to accomplish these two objectives. It is an excellent example of cooperative efforts designed to affect preschool children in a positive manner. Finally, I provide a personal example that involved results similar to those achieved by PAT and First Steps. In one of my districts, we developed preschool kits that were loaned out to parents of special-education students. The kits contained everything from puzzles to books to crayons to musical tapes, and could be used by the parents for as long as they wished. The results were students better prepared for school when they entered our formal programs.

Many examples of quality preschool programs exist, but one special one was mentioned by *The American School Board Journal*, the High/Scope Perry Preschool in Ypsilanti, Michigan. This preschool has existed for many years and is credited with increasing children's I.Q. scores by an average of 23 points. Investments of this nature pay off for schools/districts a few years later. The trouble, of course, is funding. With so many pressures on getting results from the children who are already in school, schools/districts have very little money remaining for preschool programs. For affluent districts with middle- to upper-income families, this is not a problem. The parents are the ones that the school/district expects to provide for the early learning opportunities. This, of course, is not the case in lower-income schools/districts. It is these very schools that must find ways of providing such early learning opportunities. Creating partnerships with other community agencies is one way of accomplishing this while also garnering as much public education funding as possible to provide to preschools and parent training programs.

Switch Elementary and Secondary School Starting Times

Much has been learned during the past 30 years about sleep patterns and the needs of children and adolescents. We have learned that the timing of sleep begins to change in early adolescence with both bedtime and rising time beginning later. Studies have also shown that although adolescents tend to sleep less as they mature, the need for optimal sleep time remains at approximately 9.25 hours per night. We also know that the need for sleep during the daytime increases during puberty. The consequences of insufficient sleep are also known. They include memory lapses, attention deficits, mood depression, and slowed reaction time. Therefore, the assumption is that students would be more alert and achievement would increase if they attended school during their optimal wake cycles. For these and other reasons, a number of medical personnel have advocated for a change in the start and end times in our public schools with the high schools starting later and the elementary schools starting earlier.

Until now, only a handful of school districts around the country have actually altered their start times based on sleep-deprivation research. The most prominent is the Minneapolis Public School District. Sufficient time has not yet elapsed to determine the effects the switch in start times has had on student achievement. Therefore, no objective, conclusive data exist as to the benefits of later start times for adolescents. However, an opinion survey was conducted by the Center for Applied Research and Educational Improvement (CAREI) at the University of Minnesota using focus groups of individuals who actually experienced the change in start times. These findings did reflect that a greater number of students were more alert for the first two periods of the day and that fewer students were drowsy or asleep during the school day. An interesting difference occurred between those students in the city and those in the suburbs. Students in the city were generally dissatisfied with the later starting time and reported they were more tired and had less time for homework and study. Suburban students, on the other hand, reported they felt less tired and felt more rested.

Until more objective evidence is available, entire school districts may wish to defer a change in start times. However, schools/districts may wish to consider one idea that has come from the CAREI study. It appears that no one starting time is best for all students. Some students may benefit from the current schedule, whereas others would appear to benefit from the later start time. Therefore, schools/districts that would provide flexibility of starting times may best accommodate a greater number of students and, thus, increase the probability of maximizing student achievement. Such flexibility could be delivered through choice schools or through choice start times within a school. Either option would provide an alternative for students who suffer ill effects because of the current traditional starting and ending times for our elementary, middle, and high schools.

Create Smaller Schools

A number of people believe that student achievement declines when schools exceed certain sizes. Usually the numbers associated with ineffectiveness are 1,000 students for middle and high schools, and 500 for elementary schools. Mary Fulton, a policy analyst for the Education Commission of the States (ECS), has asserted that the commission's recent report, *The ABC's of Investing in Student Performance*, indicates that small schools have higher test scores; lower absenteeism, drop-out rates and vandalism; better student attitudes and student–faculty relationships; and stronger relationships with the parents and community.

Mary Anne Raywid, a professor at Hofstra University and an expert on small schools who has written on the movement to create smaller schools, concurs with ECS. She claims that small schools have fewer discipline problems, lower drop-out rates, higher levels of student engagement and participation, better progress toward graduation, and more achievement. She also gives a rationale for why she believes this happens. It is not the size of the school by itself that creates these positive changes but the sense of community that the smaller size engenders. People can be more personal and more responsive to the needs of students, parents, and teachers. But, even deeper than this sense of community, is the sense of identification and affiliation by everyone involved in the school that creates the benefits.

Of course, it sounds easy to create small schools, and, if you are building school buildings from scratch, it is relatively easy. But what about schools that have already been constructed that are larger than the recommended sizes? Is it too late for them? The answer is "no." In cases where schools greatly exceed the recommended sizes, it is possible to create multiple small schools within a school that are distinctive and different and that afford all of the advantages that smaller school size brings. Of course, many public schools have attempted to create smallness through "houses" or "families" within the larger school. This may also work just as well, but experts like Raywid claim that it is important to make the smaller schools within a school as distinctive as possible. It is this distinctiveness that provides the sense of community and belonging that is so important.

Regardless of whether a school is built from the ground up as a small-size school, or whether an already established large school creates distinctive schools within a school, or whether a larger school creates smaller "houses" within itself, or if schools need to be built large for economic reasons, serious consideration should be given to creating small "school environments" to increase student achievement.

7

Undertake an Achievement Audit

What is the first (or next) step that a school/district can take to determine what it should do to substantially increase student achievement? An achievement audit is one answer. An achievement audit is an independent examination of the design, operations, procedures, personnel, restrictions, and processes in place that support or hamper student achievement. It is an independent, honest appraisal of how well the school/district is doing in maximizing student achievement. An achievement audit is appropriate for schools/districts that are already doing well but want to do better, schools/districts whose students are not performing well on recognized objective assessment measures, and schools/districts in between these two extremes. It is for schools/districts that are under legislative or local pressure to have students perform better, as well as for those whose parents/patrons are currently satisfied. In essence, it is for any school/district that wants the best for its students and parents and that wants its students to perform better than they currently are.

An achievement audit needs to be conducted by an outside, independent organization that understands all of the ramifications of what is required to increase achievement. The organization needs to have the trained personnel, techniques, processes, experience, and instruments to provide an accurate portrayal of the assets a school/district already possesses and of the alternative choices that would lead to increased student achievement. The organization should be able to provide ongoing assistance and training to the school/district to the degree the school/district desires in specific areas, or in support of recommendations, the school/district has selected to implement from the report provided by the organization.

An independent organization is important for a number of reasons. First, it provides credibility. It demonstrates that the school/district is serious about improving student achievement. It demonstrates the school's/district's commitment to improvement. It eliminates any suspicion that critics may have that the school/district will do what it has already predetermined it wants to do. It also provides credibility to findings and recommendations made in the area of student achievement in the same way that a financial audit provides creditability to the actions taken or that need to be taken in the financial area.

Second, the steps that often need to be taken to increase student achievement may not be popular with a number of different politically influential groups or people. If a school/district was to make such recommendations by itself, the likelihood of the recommendation ever becoming reality is greatly diminished. The weight that independent experts can give to such controversial recommendations is simply far greater than any school/district can generate by itself.

Third, an independent achievement audit can provide a clearer picture to the leaders and participants of a school/district. The old adage that it is sometimes difficult to see the forest for the trees is often true. A look from an independent organization with a different lens, with a different way of viewing the world, and with no predisposed biases or prejudices about the school/district, can often provide a clearer picture of reality.

Any number of organizations may be appropriate for assisting schools/districts, but only one can conduct an achievement audit based on the findings in this book. That organization is The Center for Achievement in Public Education (CAPE). An achievement audit by CAPE is an extensive process that analyzes the normal operations of a school or district against every achievement element identified in *Achievement Now!*, notes the presence or absence of each factor, and then rates the strength or weakness of each element present in the school or district. The audit team may be comprised of 1 to 20 or more members depending on the size of the school or district. A fairly large number of documents are required to be sent to the Center prior to the audit in order for a preparatory examination of the achievement factors to be conducted. The team leader communicates in detail with the principal or superintendent before any audit activity is initiated. Depending on the desires of the school or district and the potential complexity of the audit, this initial communication may or may not occur on-site. The purpose of this meeting is for the audit leader to get a sense of the depth (if any) of an achievement gap and to learn of any problems the school or district may be experiencing that the school or district leader feels may be contributing to an achievement gap or that may be causing specific elements to be missing or weak. Finally, the initial meeting provides an opportunity for the principal or superintendent to emphasize any particular school or district characteristics that he/she feels are strengths, as well as any of the *Achievement Now!* achievement elements that are absent or weak because of local customs, beliefs, or sensitivities and that it may be best to minimize or avoid in an audit.

Following this preparatory document work and initial communication meeting, an on-site visit is made to the school or district. The on-site visit may last from 3 to 20 days, again depending on the size of the school/district. The on-site visit is comprised of school and classroom observations and extensive teacher, administrator, student, and parent interviews, as well as a review of more paper documents. If the audit is a district audit, a number of schools are visited and interviews are extended to board members and more central administrators along with the superintendent and cabinet.

Following the on-site visit, the audit team undertakes an extensive analysis of the data they collected. These data permit the team to determine of the presence or absence of each achievement element and the strength of each element that is found. A detailed draft report is prepared from this analysis. This draft report contains the following sections:

- *Basis of Audit*—An overall introduction or basis for the audit that uses *Achievement Now!* as the theoretical and research underpinning.

- *Sources and Techniques Used*—A detailing of the sources the audit team gathered and the techniques they used to make its determinations.

- *Achievement Elements*—Specific information found regarding each achievement element, as well as the rating of each element.

- *Commendations*—A section that lists the achievement elements or other factors that the audit team found that deserve special mention or commendation.

- *Recommendations*—A section that recommends steps that the school or district can take that should increase student achievement. These are also identified as critically (essential), strongly, moderately, or mildly recommended.

- *Executive Summary*—A short summary that can be used by policy or decision makers or for public release to the press, parents, community members, or other groups the school or district would like to inform.

The draft report is then shared with the principal or superintendent for review, correction of inaccurate or false factual information, and comment on anything from tone to recommendations. The draft report is then altered to the degree possible to accommodate the principal's or superintendent's comments while maintaining the objectivity, veracity, and forthrightness that an audit requires. A number of copies of the final report are then sent to the school or district.

To complete the audit process, a final on-site visit is made by the audit leader, who will report to, and meet with, the board of education, the central administration, the school administration, the faculty, parents, and the media, depending on the desires of the principal or superintendent.

To provide a better sense of the thoroughness of an achievement audit conducted by the Center the specific factors that are included in an audit are listed below.

List of Factors Included
in an Achievement Audit

♦ Focused mission statement

♦ Guiding questions

♦ Defined core academic areas

♦ Minimum time requirement spent on core for elementary, middle, and high school

♦ Purpose of noncore areas

♦ Uninterrupted time of core academic areas

♦ Effects of noncore areas on core academic areas

♦ Length of school day for elementary, middle, and high school

♦ Length of year for elementary, middle, and high school

♦ Academic summer-school program

♦ Before/after-school program

♦ Before/after-school program coordinated to school academic program

♦ Nonschool tutorial programs

♦ In-school tutorial programs

♦ Homework policy requirement

♦ Quality of homework

♦ Completion percentage of homework

♦ Homework—nonclass time-completion requirement

♦ Length of homework grading time

♦ Quantity of homework for elementary, middle, and high school

♦ Graduation requirements for the core academic areas of English, science, mathematics, social studies, foreign language, core electives, and total core

♦ Graduation requirements for the noncore academic areas of physical education and the arts

♦ Graduation requirements for unrestricted electives

♦ Frequency of assemblies, special days, and special events

♦ Academic nature of assemblies, special days, and special events

♦ Quality of substitute lesson plans for substitute teachers

♦ After-school reading programs and incentives

♦ Student attendance for elementary, middle, and high school

♦ Standards-based approach

♦ Alignment of vertical curriculum

♦ Elementary foreign language

♦ Completion percentage of middle-school student body for algebra, geometry, foreign language, biology, and other advanced subjects

♦ Completion percentage of high-school student body of 1–2, 3–4, and 5+ Advanced Placement (AP) courses

♦ Percentage of high-school students taking AP courses that score 3 or above

♦ Internationale Baccalaureate program for elementary, middle, and high school

♦ Online advanced course availability

♦ Policy for regression to easier subjects

♦ Assessment aligned to curriculum

♦ Grade inflation—expected versus actual GPA for school

♦ Research-proven curriculum

♦ Weighted grades

- Student discipline
- Student decorum and general school order
- Zero-tolerance policy
- School-wide rules
- School uniforms
- Established set of values taught to students
- Student engagement
- Whole-language policy
- Inclusion of phonics in reading instruction
- Thoroughness of grammar, spelling, and conventions
- Developmentalism policy
- Appropriateness of kindergarten reading
- Appropriateness of kindergarten mathematics
- Basic mathematical computation policy
- Specific/direct instruction in basic mathematical computation
- Appropriate use of calculators
- Multiple intelligences policy
- Middle school philosophy policy
- Direct reading instruction for all students in middle school
- Adequate middle school writing instruction
- Appropriateness of home economics and technology shop classes
- Accountability evaluation policy
- Accountability evaluations for superintendent, principals, central and other administrators, teachers, and support staff
- Staff acceptance of accountability
- Results orientation
- High-stakes assessment
- Financial incentives for achievement

- Competition policy
- Academic charter schools
- Academic magnet/focus schools
- Whole-school reform models
- Restructured traditional schools
- Homeschool support
- Collaborative change process when possible
- Forced change when necessary
- Percentage of acceptance of need for change by teachers/staff, administrators, and board members
- Percentage of belief in change by teachers/staff, administrators, and board members
- Site-based management policy
- District decision matrix
- School decision matrix
- PPOR funding mechanism
- Percentage of teachers with students outperforming objective expectations
- Substitute teacher quality
- Middle school teacher certification in mathematics and science
- Limited but enforced rules
- Anti-bullying program
- Staff development—combined teacher/school/district model
- Dollars spent on staff development
- Percentage of parental involvement in PTA/PTO, volunteer assignments, and attendance at report-card meetings, athletic/extracurricular activities, and special events for elementary, middle, and high school
- Class size for primary, intermediate, middle, and high-school grade levels

- Preschool program for three- to four-year-olds, zero to two years old, and prenatal
- School start time for elementary, middle, and high school
- School size for elementary, middle, and high school
- Schools within schools

As can be seen from the list, the number of elements is extensive and provides the basis for a thorough, comprehensive, and systemic review and report of all the major, known elements that affect student achievement. Such a report can provide principals, superintendents, faculties, and boards of education with a clear roadmap of steps they can take to dramatically increase student performance in a short period of time.

The Center for Achievement in Public Education

The Center for Achievement in Public Education (CAPE) was founded by the author of this book, Dr. Donald J. Fielder, as an organization devoted to assisting schools and school districts in their efforts to improve public education by dramatically increasing student achievement. Don is the president. The Center is staffed by individuals who have been highly successful in producing improved student performance in their work in public education, whether that is at the school or district level. A wealth of talent and skill is available through the Center from actual practitioners who have weathered the storms of public dissatisfaction with its public schools and the turmoil that often accompanies the changes that are necessary to improve student learning in demonstrable ways. The people in the Center are sensitive to the needs of their school and district partners as well as the needs of the students, parents, teachers, and administrators who serve our public schools so well.

Dr. Fielder and the CAPE consulting group specializes in achievement audits as well as a number of speaking programs, seminars and ongoing consulting in areas designed to improve student achievement. For more information contact:

The Center for Achievement in Public Education
Voice and Fax: 770-682-0036
E-mail: achievementnow@aol.com

Bibliography

American Association of School Administrators. (1999). *An educators' guide to schoolwide reform*. Arlington, VA: Author.

Anderson, J. (1994) *Study*. Washington, DC: Office of Educational Research and Improvement, United States Department of Education.

Boyer, E. L. (1995). *The basic school: A community for learning*. San Francisco: Jossey-Bass.

Brigham, S. E. (1994). TQM: Lessons we can learn from industry. In *Quality goes to school*. Arlington, VA: American Association of School Administrators.

Bushweller, K. (1997, September). Teaching to the test. *The American School Board Journal,184*(9), 20–25.

Carskadon, M. A. (1999, January). When worlds collide: Adolescent need for sleep versus societal demands. *Phi Delta Kappan, 80*(5),348–353.

Cawelti, G. (1999, July). Improving achievement: Finding research-based practices and programs that boost student achievement. *The American School Board Journal, 186*(7), 34–37.

Chase, B. (2002, May). *All in the family: Educating our children in post-September 11 America*, Speech made before the National Press Club, Washington, DC.

Clinchy, E. (1995, Winter) The changing nature of our magnet schools. *New Schools, New Communities, 11*(2), 47–50.

Colvin, R. L. (1999, January). Math wars: Tradition vs. real-world applications. *The School Administrator, 56*(1)26–31.

Coonradt, C. A., & Nelson, L. (1991). *The game of work: How to enjoy work as much as play*. Salt Lake City, UT: Shadow Mountain.

Darling-Hammond, L. (2000). Teacher quality and student achievement: A review of state policy evidence. *Education Policy Analysis Archives, 8*(1).

Deal, T. E., & Peterson, K. D. (1994). *The leadership paradox: Balancing logic and artistry in schools.* San Francisco: Jossey-Bass.

Deming, W. E. (1986). *Out of the crisis.* Cambridge, MA: Massachusetts Institute of Technology Center for Advanced Engineering Study.

Deming, W. E. (1993). *The new economics for industry, government, education.* Cambridge, MA: Massachusetts Institute of Technology Center for Advanced Engineering Study.

Drake, J. M. (1981). Making effective use of the substitute teacher: An administrative opportunity. *NASSP Bulletin, 65,* 74–80.

Duffey, J. (1999, March). Home school–public school partnerships. *Curriculum Report, 28*(4), 1–4.

EduVentures. (1999). *The education industry: Markets and opportunities.* Boston: Author.

Edwards, V. B. (Ed.). (1999, January). Quality counts'99: Rewarding results, punishing failure. *Education Week, XVIII*(17), 1–206.

Eisner, E. W. (1988). *The role of discipline-based art education in America's schools.* J. Paul Getty Trust.

English, F. W. (1988). *Curriculum auditing.* Lancaster, PA: Technomic.

Fielder, D. J. (1989). *An examination of substitute teacher effectiveness.* Doctoral dissertation study, Vanderbilt University, Nashville, TN.

Fielder, D. J. (1991, April). Allowing schools to hire staff. *The School Administrator,* 35.

Fielder, D. J. (2002). *The leadership teachings of Geronimo: How 19 defeated 5000.* Pittsburg, PA: CeShore SterlingHouse.

Fielding, L., Kerr, N., & Rosier, P. (1998). *The 90 percent reading goal.* Kennewick, WA: The New Foundation Press.

Friedman, N. L. (1983). High school substituting: Task demands and adaptations in educational work. *Urban Education, 18,* 114–126.

Garfield, C. A. (1986). *Peak performers*. New York: William Morrow.

Godwin, R. K., & Kemerer, F. R. (2002, May 15). School choice trade-offs. *Education Week, XXI*(36), 39, 52.

Goldhaber, D. D., & Brewer, D. J. (1996). Evaluating the effect of teacher degree level on educational performance. In W. Fowler, *Developments in school finance* (pp. 97–535). Washington, DC: National Center for Education Statistics.

Good, T. L. (1981, February). Teacher expectations and student perceptions: A decade of research. *Educational Leadership, XXXVIII*(5), 415–421.

Hardy, L. (1999, April). A private solution. *The American School Board Journal, 186*(4), 46–48.

Hirsch, E. D. (1996). *The schools we need and why we don't have them*. New York: Doubleday.

Jensen, E. (1998). *Teaching with the brain in mind*. Alexandria, VA: Association for Supervision and Curriculum Development.

Jones, R. (1998). What works: Researchers tell what schoos must do to improve student achievement. *The American school Board Journal, 185*(4), 28–33.

Koretz, D. M., & Berends, M. (2001). *Changes in high school grading standards in mathematics 1982–1992*. Santa Monica, CA: The Rand Corporation.

Kroeze, D. J., & Johnson, D. P. *Achieving excellence: A report of initial findings of eighth grade performance from the third international mathematics and science study*. Oak Brook, IL: North Central Regional Laboratory for the First in the World Consortium.

Kubow, P. K., Wahlstrom, K. L., & Bemis, A. E. (1999, January). Starting time and school life: Reflections from educators and students. *Phi Delta Kappan, 80*(5)366–371.

Martin, M., Mullis, I., Gonzalez, E., O'Connor, K., Chrostowski, S., Gregory, K., et al. (2001). *Science benchmarking report: TIMSS 1999— Eighth grade*. Boston: International Study Center, Lynch School of Education.

McNally, D. (1990). *Even eagles need a push: Learning to soar in a changing world.* New York: Dell.

Mullis, I. V. S., Mullis, I., Gonzalez, E., O'Connor, K., Chrostowski, S., Gregory, K., et al. (2001). *Mathematics benchmarking report: TIMSS 1999—Eighth grade.* Boston: International Study Center, Lynch School of Education.

Murphy, J., & Schiller, J. (1992). *Transforming America's schools: An administrators' call to action.* La Salle, IL: Open Court.

National Center for Educational Statistics. (1988). *National education longitudinal study of 1988.* Washington, DC: Author.

National Center for Educational Statistics. (2002). *The condition of education, 2000.* Washington, DC: Author.

National Coalition for Parent Involvement in Schools. (2002). *The benefits of family–school partnerships.* Fairfax, VA: Author.

Odden, A. (1998). *Financing schools for high performance: Strategies for improving the use of educational resources.* San Francisco: Jossey-Bass.

Peak, L. (1996). *Pursuing excellence: A study of U. S. eight-grade mathematics and science teaching, learning, curriculum, and achievement in international context.* Washington, DC: National Center for Education Statistics, Office of Educational Research and Improvement, U. S. Department of Education.

Project Appleseed. (2002). *The parental involvement checklist.* St. Louis, MO: Author.

Project Appleseed. (2002). *The six standards of parental involvement.* St. Louis, MO: Author.

Public Agenda. (1998). *Reality check.* New York: Author.

Public Agenda. (1999). *Playing their parts.* New York: Author.

Raywid, M. A. (1997, October). Successful school downsizing. *The School Administrator, 54*(9), 18–23.

Report of the National Education Commission on Time and Learning. (1994). *Prisoners of time.* Washington, DC: Author.

Rosovsky, H., & Hartley, M. (2002). *Evaluation and the academy: Are we doing the right thing? Grade inflation and letters of recommendation.* Cambridge, MA: American Academy of Arts and Sciences.

Sanders, W. L., & Horn, S. P. (1998). Research findings from the Tennessee Value-Added Assessment System (TVAAS) database: Implications for educational evaluation and research. *Journal of Personnel Evaluation in Education, 12*(3), 247–256.

Schlechty, P. C. (1990). *Schools for the 21st Century,* San Francisco: Jossey–Bass.

Schmidt, W. H., McKnight, C. C., & Raizen, S. A. (1996). *A splintered vision: An investigation of U. S. science and mathematics education.* East Lansing, MI: U. S. National Research Center for the Third International Mathematics and Science Study.

Schmoker, M. (1996). *Results: The key to continuous school improvement.* Alexandria, VA: Association for Supervision and Curriculum Development.

Schwahn, C. J., & Spady, W. G. (1998). *Total leaders: Applying the best future–focused change strategies to education.* Arlington, VA: American Association of School Administrators.

Snow, C. E., Burns, M. S., & Griffin, P. (Eds.). (1998). *Preventing reading difficulties in young children* (Committee on the Prevention of Reading Difficulties in Young Children, National Research Council). Washington, DC: National Academy Press.

Steel, L., & Levine, R. (1994). *Educational innovation in multiracial contexts: The growth of magnet schools in American education.* Washington, DC: American Institutes for Research for the U. S. Department of Education.

Takahira, S., Gonzalez, P., Frase, M., Salganik, L. H. (1998). *Pursuing excellence: A study of U. S. twelfth-grade mathematics and science achievement in international context.* Washington, DC: National Center for Educational Statistics, Office of Educational Research and Improvement, U.S. Department of Education.

The ABC's of investing in student performance. Denver, CO: Education Commission of the States.

Fulton, M. (1996). *The Book of Knowledge*. (1999). New York: Merrill Lynch.

The Education Trust. (1996). *Education Watch: The 1997 education trust state and national data book*. Washington, DC: Author.

Vance, M., & Deaton, D. (1997). *Think Out of the Box*. Franklin Lakes, NJ: Career Press.

What works: Research about teaching and learning. (1987). Washington, DC: U. S. Department of Education.

Williamson, R. D., & Johnston, J. H. (1998, August). The fate of middle schooling. *The School Administrator, 55*(7), 30–33.